The Expert's Job Seeking Methods

The Expert's Job Seeking Methods

Success through Proven Techniques

- Job Seeking Skills
- Interviewing Skills
- Resume' Writing Skills
- Letter Writing Skills
- and more.

We Will Teach You How

Gerald N. Calandra, Ed.D., J.D.

ARCHWAY PUBLISHING

Archway Publishing books may be ordered through booksellers or by contacting:

Archway Publishing
1663 Liberty Drive
Bloomington, IN 47403
www.archwaypublishing.com
1-(888)-242-5904

Because of the dynamic nature of the Internet, any web addresses or links contained in this book may have changed since publication and may no longer be valid. The views expressed in this work are solely those of the author and do not necessarily reflect the views of the publisher, and the publisher hereby disclaims any responsibility for them.

Any people depicted in stock imagery provided by Thinkstock are models, and such images are being used for illustrative purposes only.
Certain stock imagery © Thinkstock.

ISBN: 978-1-4808-0873-7 (sc)
ISBN: 978-1-4808-0874-4 (e)

Library of Congress Control Number: 2014911328

Printed in the United States of America.

Archway Publishing rev. date: 09/22/2014

The Laurel Wreath first appeared in Greek mythology both in athletic competitions and poetic meets. It was awared to the victors at the Ancient Olympic Games and represented the highest level of achievement.

Acknowledgements

To my Mother and Father who guided me whenever they could and to my wife Carolyne whose support and encouragement has been steadfast and faithful.

CONTENTS

Part I Starting Your Job Search

Part II Initial Contact

Part III Social Media

Part IV Interviewing Skills

PART 1

Starting Your Job Search

WELCOME

Finding a job, starting a career, or advancing a career in today's world is not easy. It's hard work, and unfortunately, it never stops! Wherever you might be on your career ladder, you will find yourself needing job-procurement techniques.

The Expert's Job-Seeking Methods will make that easy for you. The book's objective is to provide you with all the tools, expertise, and skills you need to go about finding that new position for yourself.

Whether you're looking for your first job, a new advanced position, or a transition from one career to another, the system outlined here will provide you with the job-seeking skills you need. You will gain self-mastery that allows you to control your job search.

You've probably heard the old saying that best describes self-mastery: "Give a man a fish and he'll eat for a day, but teach a man to fish and he'll eat for a lifetime."

The Expert's Job-Seeking Methods will teach you how to get the job you are seeking by using the proper mechanics and techniques yourself. In our fast-changing workplace, finding a job can be a very tedious process. However, for those who have the tools, for those who have the expertise, and for those who have the desire, the process can be very easy.

Anything can be easy and rewarding when you know how to do it! The goal of *The Expert's Job-Seeking Methods* is to get you to that place of mastery with your job-seeking efforts.

INTRODUCTION

Everywhere we turn, we are faced with unstable economic conditions. The job and employment scene has become more and more difficult. In the United States, the total workforce far outnumbers the positions available for any level of employment. Obtaining a job, any job, has become increasingly challenging.

Not since the Great Depression has our country or the world faced a similar crisis. Unemployment levels are the highest they have been since the 1930s. Costs of goods and services are skyrocketing, and nearly all economic conditions are at the breaking point.

From low-level manual laborers to high-level white-collar executives, not a single group, male or female, blue-collar or white-collar, is exempt from this predicament. That is why it has become essential to learn and utilize specialized job-procurement skills. These unique skills will allow you to acquire the highest results in job procurement, job security, and career advancement. These skills can become a lifelong strategy that allows you to utilize your education, experience, and background to the fullest.

Regardless of the nature of your job or the level of your career. you will be able to use the strategies you learn from *The Expert's Job-Seeking Methods*. This will help you advance and/or maintain the highest-level job and career position possible.

In today's marketplace, rarely do employers come looking for you. This would seem like a seller's market because companies have a limited number of jobs available "for sale" and are therefor able to pick candidates from a large pool of interested and competitive individuals. Actually, this situation is ideal, because it means that when you get the job you will have proven you're the best. Let *The Expert's Job Seeking Methods* teach you how.

Job-seeking, however, is no longer a haphazard affair. *The Expert's Job-Seeking Methods* provides you with a huge advantage over the competition in landing that job offer you're looking for. This system produces repeatable results and has a history of not only advancing careers but of leading people into completely new career directions. This book offers you the foundational strategy to generate an advantage in your career and life.

JOB SEEKING METHODS

After many years of job-seeking and helping countless other individuals find jobs, I know the importance of giving something back and paying forward. This chapter will provide you with a fresh perspective that encompasses many more unique avenues than the average methodology of job-seeking.

In the perspectives, explanations, and descriptions presented here, you will learn about numerous types of job-seeking and job-procurement situations from the *affective* and *effective* standpoint. This type of approach gives you an advantage over average job-seekers—others like you who are out there looking, hunting, and yes, even grasping for a job.

By now, you may be asking what I mean by *affective* vs. *effective.* You will want to encompass both of these approaches to job-seeking. To *affect* something is to have feelings for something. If you are affected by something, you are influenced or acted upon or emotionally moved or touched. When you are affective toward someone or something, you have made an impression, or you have influenced, or you have directed that someone or something. As you can see, *affect* is usually a verb.

On the other hand, *effect* means the power or ability to bring about positive results. When you are effective, you are in one place and make progress from where you were beforehand. You demonstrate not merely potential or theoretical outcomes but results that are concrete and distinct. Being effective means you are producing a desired or a definite result. In this case, *effect* is usually a noun meaning "result."

This sentence should help you differentiate the two meanings: "Drinking affects driving, while drinking has a bad effect on driving."

The job-seeking methods presented here will come from both an affective and an effective standpoint—affective in terms of making a good impression or influencing or directing someone and effective in terms of showing you how to become capable of bringing about desired, definite, and positive results. We will teach you this skill along with many others, including résumé writing, letter writing, telephoning, interviewing, and job acceptance.

The Expert's Job-Seeking Methods does not just teach you how to write a résumé or a cover letter. It guides you step-by-step through a strategic plan that gives you a huge advantage over your competition. Knowing what to do and how to do it will put you into this valued position. This advantage can be used to find a new job, get a promotion, and even make a complete career change.

At the completion of this program you will be in a position to control your own job-seeking, job advancement, and job fulfillment. Each step you take from then on will only be to your advantage in the job-procurement process.

N.B.: Additional information may be obtained by attending one of my Job Seeking Seminars. These seminars are held in various parts of the USA throughout the year. In session one, I spend approximately two to three hours lecturing completely on the materials covered in my manual. All aspects of the manual are addressed with emphasis on individual attention to job seeking skills. In session two I spend two to three more hours working with you to aid in development of your own personal job seeking skills. None of our groups are more than 40 participants in size so that each individual gets the personal attention they need.

My specially arranged consultation can also be scheduled and spent working individually with you on a one-to-one basis in development of skills for your total personal job seeking package.

Check with my website at www.jobseekingskills.com for further information and clarification.

OVERVIEW

A few years ago, a typical expectation for job-seekers in the hunt for a new position was that it would take at least one month for every $10,000 in salary the seeker expected in the offer. In other words, if you were seeking a $50,000-a-year position, it would take at least five months.

Today, in the current economic and job environment, that number has at least doubled, and in some industries, it has tripled. What once took five months can now take ten to fifteen months to land what is now a $150,000-a-year position. This is why you need a plan, a system, and a direction to keep you focused and on track.

The most important thing for you to remember as you embark on this journey and effort to find the right job is to be patient! You should expect to be working at this process for a number of months. You will learn a lot about yourself and the job market from this experience. In addition, you should also develop a number of good relationships along the way. These relationships may not result in a job today, but they could very well help you in the future, so be certain to plug them into your networking file.

This process is an investment in your future—and like any worthwhile investment, it will take time to pay off.

YOUR MIND-SET

So here you are. You've lost your job, and you have no idea what's going to happen next. Or you've just graduated from college, and you have no idea where you are going to start looking for a job. Or you've worked hard to get to a high-level executive position and you, too, are out of a job. All you've been reading and hearing about is how bad the job market is today—how anyone who finds a job today is just plain lucky.

At my high-school graduation, many moons ago, the superintendent of schools made a statement in a speech that I still remember today. It went something like this: "Wherever you go or whatever you do in life, you make your own luck."

I have never forgotten this statement. I remember him going on and explaining how *you* were the only one responsible for your own luck. You were in complete control of your own luck. You were the one, the only one, who had any say in your own luck.

After so many years, I realize the truth in this statement. No matter what you do in life, you are the one, the only one who controls your luck. You might even say this luck in turn controls your destiny.

GETTING CREATIVE

Maybe you're convinced that bad luck is responsible when you experience setbacks like the following:

» The economy is bad and your company had to downsize in order to stay in existence and you lost your job.

» You happened to graduate from college in a year when the market was flooded with people who had the same major, resulting in very few available jobs.

» You worked hard for thirty years or more to achieve a high level of executive management and now the company has replaced you with a much younger person, at much less pay, so you are out of a job.

Certainly, these are all unfortunate circumstances, and all out of your control. But what are you going to do about it? Go to the local pub, cry in your beer, and hope someone feels sorry for you? Sit at home and watch the few soap operas that have not yet been cancelled hoping someone will come knocking at your door offering you the job you wish you had or think you deserve? Take it out on the cat, your family, or your friends, making everybody else miserable too?

No! No! No! This will get you nowhere!

You need to create a positive mind-set, develop new skills, and change your approach. Get yourself a new outlook and a new attitude. Look at the opportunities that are available. You need to change your whole way of thinking about your situation, evaluating your prospects, and going after a job.

I have seen way too many individuals go into deep depression, get very angry, feel very sorry for themselves, and become very hopeless about their existence. They might think this is the way for them to go, but it certainly will not solve the problem of finding a job.

So what do you do when you've been out there for three months, six months, maybe even a year or more looking for a job? Your savings, if you even had any, are slowly dwindling. Your parents or your spouse are getting anxious about your sitting around the house feeling sorry for yourself and your inability to find a job. Your personal image, your feelings of competence, your ambition itself are being tested, day in and day out.

As those who have been in the same situation will all tell you, it's a terrible way to wake up every morning and an even worse way to go to bed every night. But guess what, folks? You are not alone! There are many others, hundreds of thousands in fact, out there in the same condition.

The difference between them and you is that *you* are here doing something about it.

There are a number of ways to get a job. Even in today's market, where there are often many more job-seekers than available jobs, you can increase your chances of being the one selected. But not all strategies are effective.

One common technique is to go to one or more of the job boards located in various places, post your résumé and credentials, and then simply sit back and wait to be contacted by an employer or placement agency. Sometimes you will even receive an e-mail from the job board itself saying that it has a possible match for you. This is one example of what we call the "hope and pray" strategy. You hope that someone will discover you, and then you pray it will be that ideal job.

Sure, it's better than sitting on your couch expecting someone to come knocking on your front door offering you a job. It is, however, way too passive for someone who is *really* looking for a job. You see, "looking" is an *action*. To be looking, you need to take action for yourself on your behalf.

Are job boards worthless? No, not at all! In fact, some employers *contract* with job boards to list their open positions and manage the application process for them. Let's just say that hope-and-pray strategies can be used to augment your job hunt, but they should not be the primary vehicle to finding your next position.

A CAREER OR A JOB

There seems to be a bit of confusion about careers and jobs. If I choose this job, does that mean forever? What if I don't like this type of career?

"Once upon a time," as they say in fairy tales, people started in a career with an organization and stayed with that organization for their entire working lives. I know, that's hard to believe, right?

Today, a person working for an organization for more than five to seven years is rare. It is expected that college graduates today will have three to five careers—yes, *careers*, and not jobs. Just because you pick up a job in one career today does not mean that you are stuck with that job or career for the rest of your life. It just means you have an opportunity to work for this organization for as long as you are both getting a benefit from the association.

A career can be a path within an organization or an industry where the traveler moves up the ladder to take on new and different responsibilities. Sometimes, a career path will be both. The career typically lasts for a number of years. Think of it like a baseball player's career. Some players have the talent and longevity to last for twenty or more years, while others play for only a season or two. In either case, the player moves on to another phase in life and sets off on another career path.

Sometimes we look back at what we have done and say, "This has been my career path." The wiser among us, though, will plan that path out ahead of time. You may know, for example, that you want to be president of your own organization and retire, or work for the state government for thirty years and retire, or be a freelance writer so you can work for various clients and finally retire.

Increasingly, today's professionals are discovering that career change is both refreshing and necessary. We have seen entire industries wiped out by technology. Not sure that's true? Look no further than travel agents, music and motion-picture distributors, and most recently book publishers. Career change is simply a matter of changing the path you are on by recasting yourself and leveraging the experience, track record, knowledge, skills, and connections gained over the years.

One way many professionals are making this career change is by going into consulting. By leveraging their experience, many midcareer knowledge-workers are connecting with employment agencies and placement companies (recruiters, placement specialists, hiring agencies, or the dreaded "headhunters" to locate contract or contract-to-hire positions.

These positions are not typically listed anywhere by the organization because it is the agency's job to locate, interview, and qualify candidates before presenting them to the organization for approval. The organization pays the agency a percentage of the contractor's pay as compensation for locating and qualifying these potential employees. If you have the experience in an in-demand field, this may be a good option to look into.

If you are just starting out on your career path, you will need to rely more heavily on your knowledge, skills, and connections. This provides you with the experience and track record to move up in the industry or change paths into another industry.

Jobs are the stops or positions along your career path that provide you with the following:

» new experiences

» new track records

» new enhanced knowledge

» new and improved skills

» new connections

» new networks

If you have worked in an organization for a number of years, you have likely been promoted and changed positions within your field. As you plan to make your next move, consider how you can improve or deepen your experiences and track record, how you can build a larger network of connections, and how you can improve your knowledge and skills.

As you assess your job opportunities, ask yourself, "How will this position add to my career and/or help better establish me in this industry?" We have found that if you can find one or two ways to get excited about your current position—ways to grow or improve—it makes seeking your new opportunity easier. There is less pressure on you personally, which puts you more in control of the process.

WHO IS HIRING?

Things are changing in the job market very quickly. There are a good number of industries and sectors that are hiring more than others. Here's a list of a few sectors considered to have solid outlooks over the next decade (in no particular order):

» *Consulting* in the management, technology, and science fields is a promising field for those with the appropriate experience.

» *Home health/senior care* workers will continue to be in high demand as the Baby Boomers age out of the workplace. Positions include RNs, LPNs, physical and massage therapists, home-care consultants, patient advocates, estate planners, and transition and end-of-life coaches and consultants.

» *Software development/system design* will continue to boom as technology becomes more and more integrated into our daily lives. Gaming and mobile-device markets are still expanding, as are online applications and the systems to support them. Positions include engineers, software designers, quality-assurance technicians, sales representatives, and business analysts.

» *Outpatient/clinic/nursing care* will continue to see high demand, as will the health-care industry as a whole. As health-care costs spiral, any industries that support home or clinic care will continue to see increasingly strong demand. This includes chiropractic and acupressure/acupuncture professionals, supply sales reps, licensed health-care providers, physical therapists, rehabilitation specialists, and physician assistants.

» *Electronic publishing* will continue to expand with the use of devices like Kindle, Nook, and others. Web-based organizations that publish, edit, create, and market these materials will also flourish. Positions include independent copywriters, authors, graphic designers, musicians, web designers, editors, proofreaders, translators, and social-media experts.

» *Online education* will grow in response to the transition in the job market, high unemployment rates, the higher cost of higher education, and government subsidies. Online universities and tech schools are booming. Instructors, consultants, administrators to run the organizations, recruiters, and financial-aid specialists are in high demand.

» *Hearing/vision/dental service providers* continue to be needed. While dealing with the insurance industry and controlling expenses is a challenge for these service providers, the demand for their services and expertise is increasing. This includes positions on the administrative staff and suppliers to the offices of these service providers.

As you look over that list, ask yourself two big questions:

1. Do any of these areas interest me or excite me?
2. How can I present my existing skills and knowledge so that they are interesting to an employer in one of these sectors?

This is how you begin to see the opportunities around you. You have an accounting degree and the accounting firms in your area are not hiring. What about the start-up software-publishing company you just read about in your local paper? Could that company use your skills? Maybe a better question to ask yourself is, "How can I present myself in such a way that they can see how much they need me?"

The opportunities are out there. You just need to look differently for them.

PART II

Initial Contact

No matter how you make contact with a potential employer, the initial contact is vital. Remember the old saying, "You never get a second chance to make a good first impression"?

In today's age of modern communication, you never get a second chance to make a good first impression, or a third chance, or so on and so on. Every impression you make must be as good as a "good first impression"!

Because everyone today has access to the Internet and anyone can obtain your résumé through the Internet, I would like to start off with your first good impression: a résumé.

THE RÉSUMÉ

More than likely, you have already developed a résumé and may have used it in various contexts. That résumé will contain many things you need in order to gain attention for yourself. Gaining attention is exactly what a résumé is designed for, and that is what you'll want to concentrate on, along with a few other things.

In many ways, a résumé is nothing more than a short one- to three-page document directing a reader's attention to all the information that is pertinent to you as a person—whether it's your background and its relevance to the particular position or your desire to provide eagerness to advance and/or maintain the same particular position. These are both very important.

Your résumé is usually your first chance to make a "good first impression." A good first impression is the manner in which you present yourself to a potential employer. You haven't much choice either, especially if it is published on the Internet through LinkedIn and the like.

Although you will have other chances to make a good first impression, this will become your most important initial opportunity. It is your first actual exposure to the outside world, and it must be perfect, impeccable, and flawless. It must prompt someone, anyone, to want to learn more about you! After all, it is the first definite impression you are making on a potential employer.

When preparing your résumé, it is vital to inspire interest in yourself and convince the potential employer to make contact with you. For this reason, your résumé must look different from one written as a catalog of your job history. Your résumé must distinctly and obviously show you are the best candidate for the job. It must show you are the best candidate to help the potential employer be effective. It must show the most positive evidence of how your abilities will help the company.

Your résumé is a record of your education, job-related experiences, extracurricular experiences, achievements, and skills. This document allows would-be employers to learn basic facts about you and your abilities far in advance of meeting you or even contacting you.

A standard résumé contains individual sections for personal details, education, and work history. Usually, résumés are organized in chronological order. The "functional résumé" is generally frowned upon by employers because it is typically used to hide long gaps in employment and frequent job changes. With large-scale downsizing and layoffs at every level, you can explain any recent gaps in your cover letter, which I will describe later.

In a chronological résumé, you show your most recent employment first and then list all of your relevant positions back from there in reverse chronological order. By *relevant*, I mean that if you are applying for a communications position at a corporation, your high-school fast-food job can be left off, unless it helps strengthen the case for the position you are seeking.

You will need to sort all jobs or positions in a work-history section. Sort these in order of the most recent first. The one exception might be when a specific job fits in more closely with the position for which you are applying. When this happens, you would definitely list the relevant position first.

One of the major mistakes you might make at this point is to simply rewrite your last job description. Aside from correct spelling and proper grammar, you must write any job description in such a way as to make you look appealing to the potential employer. You can do this by telling potential employers how you can specifically help them. Explain previous situations by showing the successes you achieved with a former employer or a former situation.

Explain what made you different from the rest and why that contributed to success for the company. Remember to be truthful and don't overhype! If you had wins like reorganization of a group into a functional team, which in turn increased production by X percent, or you helped get the company e-newsletter successfully online for the six months prior to your departure, use those experiences! You are looking to highlight accomplishments and achievements that explain how you will be a benefit to your potential employers.

You must make yourself look like a problem-solver, a self-motivated person, someone who carries any task to completion. This will be your opportunity to let the potential employer know how dedicated you are in what you are assigned to complete. A great deal of thought and effort needs to be put into this part of your résumé in order to make it happen and make it a success. You need to be thinking, "What can I do to help or bring value to my prospective employer?"

Regardless of what entry-level position you are looking for, you must think in such a way as to show what you achieved in your past experience, internships, paid work, or volunteer work. This is true for entry-level positions for those just out of college; middle-level positions for those looking for new jobs; any type of advancement, lateral movement, or career change; and executive positions.

Think in terms of what you achieved for your current school, current employer, or previous employer. What proficiencies, competencies, or skills did you learn that will make you valuable in the position for which you are now applying? What skills are valuable to this potential employer? Demonstrate them by showing how you were chosen previously to perform a specific skill and what accomplishments you achieved. For example:

On more than one occasion, I was asked to develop production plans that would improve performance, advance goals, and satisfy the economic needs of our company and its employees. In each instance, they were developed and completed. Their success was a direct result of my input and efforts, and they brought about considerable improvement in production, enhancement, and profitability for the company overall.

I cannot stress how important a résumé is in any job search. The résumé should be designed to get you an interview with the potential employer. As a rule of thumb, it should not be more than two typewritten pages. It should contain in a brief format all of the information prospective employers will need to know about you and how you can best meet their needs.

You will use certain techniques to create a résumé that will get the interviewer's attention. They include the following:

» Bullets like these to assist the reader in seeing your excellent achievements.

» White spaces and fonts to focus your reader's attention on desired activities.

» Action words and phrases that point out you are a positive, self-motivated, accomplished individual.

The résumé should be specific to the job. If you need to write a separate résumé for each separate job—if each separate job is different—then do it! It is worth the effort, and it will pay off in the end. This résumé will need to motivate the employer to meet you. It must set you apart from all the other applicants and make the employer want you above the rest. That's why it *must* be specific to each job.

Presenting a strong picture of your abilities to a potential employer means fully answering the following questions:

» Why are you different from other candidates competing for the same position?

» Why are your accomplishments thus far in your career so significant?

» What traits or talents make you truly unique?

» What notable personal character traits make you the best candidate for this position?

» What problem-solving challenges have you met that will be beneficial to a potential employer?

The résumé is definitely a serious presentation and a selling tool. It identifies you and makes you stand out to recruiters and potential employers. It opens doors to opportunities and possibilities. If your résumé works, you get the interview, and *you* work! If the résumé doesn't work, neither do you. It is the most essential, critical, and crucial document you will ever put together.

We feel it is best to start out in any employment situation with a simple two-page résumé. If done properly, it will present you as far and away the best person for the job.

Résumés containing keywords make you stand out from the crowd and make you more desirable to potential employers. These keywords are nothing more than active verbs that put you in a favorable or flattering light. Appendix D contains a listing of active verbs you can use as keywords in your résumé and letters.

THE PROFILE

Because an increasing number of job-seekers and employers are using Internet-based job-search engines to find and fill employment positions, the rules have changed somewhat. For this reason, a long résumé may be less desirable than a short, concise, one-page profile. I am seeing profiles being used much more frequently prior to a complete résumé.

This does not mean, however, that a résumé is no longer important. It just means the profile becomes a *shorter* version of the résumé. I still encourage developing a résumé because it creates the foundation for your job-application process.

Profiles allow employers to quickly go through many more applications and have many more choices available in their search. For this reason, it becomes even more important that you use keywords to describe yourself—keywords that do the following:

» pertain to the qualifications needed for the job

» describe you in a favorable light

» point out your superior qualifications

The important point is to get the potential employer interested in you. Using the keywords pertinent to the job will attract potential employers to you.

Developing a profile containing keywords is very, very important. You can find examples of profiles in the appendices along with résumés, motivating letters, and keywords.

MORE RÉSUMÉS

Developing a résumé is still the first step in preparation for a job. It is a basic foundation for your job search. A résumé, if done properly, gives you all the necessary tools to go ahead and develop any other type of document used in your job-seeking process.

With the résumé developed first, you can then go on to develop your profile, your motivating letter, and any of your follow-up letters needed for the job-seeking process. Your résumé should include these five elements:

1. Contact information
2. Job objective
3. Experience
4. Competencies
5. Education

Nearly every position you apply for is going to be somewhat different. Therefore, each résumé or profile you submit will also be somewhat different. However, they all need to be based on the same skills and accomplishments.

Please note that, in today's world, you can no longer have two résumés that contradict each other. A background check, before or after you are hired, may uncover the discrepancies and could cost you the offer or the job. Don't get caught in the trap of creating falsehoods to obtain an interview.

Gear each résumé specifically to the job for which you are applying. By all means, use the same format. It will be to your advantage for each résumé to be tailored to the specific responsibilities of the position for which you are applying. This is why we do not suggest that you shotgun your résumé to fifty different places with a generic cover letter. Finding a job is a special process, and it takes time and effort to be successful.

THERE ARE NO SHORTCUTS TO SUCCESS

You'll want to present your types of experience, your achievements, and your education and training in the most beneficial way. Leverage your education, experience, and background so they highlight how you are a good fit for the specific position being offered.

In the appendices, you can find examples to help you organize the information concerning your education, experience, and background. Following these examples will save you time in assembling your résumé and creating the letters you will need later in the program.

If you have previous résumés, these examples will help you to bring your résumé up to date. If your résumé is up to date, you will simply fill in any additional details in each section of the new résumé.

Now let's take a look at each section of the résumé outline.

CONTACT INFORMATION

The first section is your contact information, including your name, address, telephone number, and e-mail address. This is standard each time and very seldom varies. If you have a temporary address you could be leaving prior to completion of the interview process—e.g., you are still in school and have a college address and a home address—be sure to list both. This is especially true if the home address is closer to the job location.

PERSONAL OBJECTIVE

The second section contains your personal objective. This is very important and can make or break your résumé. This objective is always found at the top of your résumé and is the first and sometimes the only thing a potential employer will see. It should be tailored to the specific position you are applying for, using the keywords from the job listing or those you have developed.

Let's imagine you're a hiring director looking to fill a position in management. You run an online ad and an ad in a local newspaper. Suddenly, you have more than 250 résumés from interested candidates. What a fantastic response!

Now you have to weed through all of these résumés to find the best candidate to fill the position. Of course, you also have regular job duties, so you are very short on time. Imagine this is you. How would you approach this daunting task?

Would you open every résumé or electronic profile and review it line by line? Having had this exact experience, I can tell you there is just no way to do that without a great deal of time and difficulty. Between the incoherent submissions and the people who obviously did not read the job requirements, any normal person quickly starts to just scan the résumés to discover and select the most suitable candidates.

What do you think a hiring director looks at first? You guessed it: your objective. For most, it becomes just like the headline in a news story. If it catches your attention, you read further. If it does not, you toss it aside. If your first impression is not good, you move on. It is all you can do to keep up with everything else. This is a prime example of why it's so important to make a good first impression.

This is why your objective needs to be tailored to the specific position for which you are applying. It should jump off of the page and make the potential employer notice you immediately. For example, let's say the first objective you write in this job search looks like this:

*Looking for a position in an organization that
can use me and give me room to grow.*

What do you think? Not much, rather boring and bland, doesn't really stand out in a crowd, probably wouldn't raise any eyebrows. How about if you write this second objective:

*Looking for a position that would use my advanced education and
extensive experience to enhance and maintain your company.*

A little bit better, but still not raising any eyebrows. This is still a résumé that is only one out of 250. Maybe it will get the attention of the potential employer, but only if there are few résumés that are better. Remember, this initial screening process typically cuts the list down to the top five or ten for further review. Now let's look at one you would definitely want to send:

*In search of a management position in Informational Technology
that utilizes my advanced experiences developing technical business
solutions to increase efficiency and maximize profitability.*

Wow! That's much better—you have targeted the situation. You are being polite while being assertive. You are being complete while being concise.

This objective is short, simple, and direct. It uses action words that mean something to the potential employer: *efficiency* and *profitability*. There are no generalizations or characterizations. The specific accomplishments, achievements, and capabilities needed to perform the job are definitely and specifically highlighted.

This is the type of objective in a résumé that gets someone's attention—by simply highlighting the skills important to the particular position.

It is important not to assume that the potential employer will read your complete résumé. You must let the potential employer know right up front what you bring to the table. Hone in on one specific objective and follow that objective through to completion. Tell about your significant successes that suited the specific situation and show just how you accomplished or achieved the specific goals.

Always, always, always emphasize accomplishments and achievements. You'll learn more about those in the next section.

EXPERIENCES, ACHIEVEMENTS, AND ACCOMPLISHMENTS

n this section, you will enter information concerning the various jobs you have held—in other words, your experience. Start with the most recent and work backward. This section should run in reverse chronological order.

Each job should be separated so that it is easy to see the transitions. Include all of the essentials: name of employer, starting date, ending date, position held, description of job, and your achievements and accomplishments while you held the position. For each position you apply for, list as much of the essential information as possible. Accuracy counts, so be specific and precise.

Including your achievements and accomplishments is critical. Explain how you attained these while working at a particular company and how these achievements and accomplishments helped the organization. Highlight the responsibilities that went along with the job as well. In many cases, a job title only describes part of what the person actually does, and in other cases, the title is so generic no one can tell what the person is responsible for achieving or accomplishing. Be sure to note what you did or are doing and how it helped or benefited the organization.

Using action words when describing your achievements and accomplishments will only help communicate your contributions to the reader better. (If you are in need of some action-word suggestions, check out the keywords in Appendix D.)

The most important thing to remember about achievements and accomplishments is that they must be pertinent and specific to the position you are seeking. Include what you have achieved and accomplished on the job and how those achievements and accomplishments helped the organization. Whenever possible, include exact numbers and specific details. Tell how you and your contributions made the organization better. Try to answer these questions about each of your previous positions:

- » How did your direct input improve profitability and efficiency?
- » How did you save the organization money?
- » How did you make your company more competitive?
- » How did you help build the company's reputation?
- » How did you help build relationships within and outside your company?
- » How did you help expand the organization's business?
- » How did you help the company fulfill its objectives?

These are some of the things you can do with your résumé to include achievements and accomplishments, and some of the points that really help sell you to an employer, but they are not job duties. Your everyday duties in a job are not achievements or accomplishments. Describe your achievements and accomplishments, but not the job duties. You must demonstrate responsibility-driven achievements and accomplishment-oriented successes.

These achievements and accomplishments show that you have initiative, you are a team player, you contribute to the organization, and you are an essential part of the organization. You want to show what you actually did in the position that was commendable. A potential employer needs to know what kind of contribution you made. Consider writing a separate sentence for each achievement and accomplishment. How does it make you different from other candidates?

CAPABILITIES

In this section, you will want to include your capabilities. These are particular skills you bring to the job. Just what you are capable of doing?

In today's very complex technology-driven society, there are basic skills you must have—skills that not only allow you to succeed in everyday living but to succeed in your profession. These include the following:

- » *Technical skills*, which are very important in our world today. They include skills required for life in general as well as any specific technical skills required for your particular job. Technical-skill development is an ongoing process, and successful people consistently improve and upgrade their skills.

- » *Interpersonal skills* are required to effectively deliver information, both verbally and nonverbally, to the people you communicate with both in and out of the job. To succeed at a high level of life and in your job, you need skills that include writing, speaking, presentation, communication, and management leadership.

- » *Psychological skills* are those you show when you have sincere concern, empathy, and interest for other people. Interaction with others is the key to psychological skills and includes the ability to help others develop and grow. If you possess psychological skills, you have the ability to create harmony when working with others; the ability to know how to motivate others; and the ability to interact with others. You increase the motivation and energy around you, and you increase your chances for success, happiness, and fulfillment in life.

EDUCATION AND TRAINING

Filling in the sections on education and training is similar to filling in the section on experience. You usually list the highest or most recent degree first and then follow in reverse chronological order. The only exception to this rule is when an earlier degree is much more similar and relevant to the job requirements. In this case, you could put the *most relevant* degree first. Then you would list the other degrees below, putting the most recent ones first.

Leave out high school if you have college or technical-school degrees. If you graduated more than twenty years ago, it might be simpler to just not put in dates. You certainly do not want your résumé discarded because you might appear too old for the job. Of course this depends upon the level of position, or whether it's your experience that makes you most qualified.

When you are listing education, if you have a relevant or significant thesis or dissertation topic, you should list the complete title. Also include any internships, awards, honors, or special recognitions you received. In some cases, it might be important to list any seminars, conferences, or special training you attended or completed. You might list your grade-point average if it's particularly high or you were in an honor society like Phi Beta Kappa. Appendix E offers some questions to make sure you think of everything you want to include:

New College Graduates

New graduates often think they have very little to offer. This is definitely not the case! If you had internships during your college career, they're all relevant, especially when they relate to the type of job you are seeking. If you worked while going to college, this is very important and very favorable. Even if you worked during the day while attending college at night to obtain a degree, this reflects favorably on your tenacity, determination, and work ethic.

We know a dentist who took six years to complete undergraduate school because he worked more than forty hours a week at a grocery store. He was able to earn an excellent grade-point average as an undergraduate student and at the same time save enough money for his first year of dental school. He entered dental school able to pay the full amount for the first year. He also received excellent grades.

We taught him how to write an attractive résumé, and using it he was able to receive enough grants, awards, and scholarships to pay for the rest of his dental-school education. Now he's a practicing dentist, and doing very well, I might add. It can be done!

Mid-Level Experience

You have now completed five to ten years on the job or in your career. You are ready to make either a lateral or an upward move within your company, or to another company, or perhaps into a completely new career. Your reasons may include the following:

- » You seek an increase in salary.
- » You seek better benefits.
- » You seek better advancement opportunities.

If your work experiences have produced a reasonable number of successes, you must emphasize these successes. On the other hand, if your education has led you to success, you must combine the education and experience leading to your success.

In either case, concentrate on the successes that put you in your present position. Be polite while being precise. List all accomplishments in a favorable light that puts you in good stead with your present employer or your potential employer. Go for it!

Executive-Level Experience

If you are at the executive level or even have a high level of work experience, you will need to concentrate on the results of your work effort. This means emphasizing the outcomes or achievements you have accomplished, including the following:

- » your results-driven work ethic
- » your years of progressive marketing experience
- » your strong general management skills in numerous areas

At this level, you would point out that you have the proven ability and experience to make an immediate positive difference for your new company in a variety of situations. You need to show how you personally delivered strong operating results by challenging all employees to seek goal-oriented objectives with incentive-based rewards. State how your expertise makes you the best qualified candidate for the position.

If you have been recruited for other positions, say so, but emphasize why this particular position is so important. At this level, you have the education, experience, and background to stand out from all the rest. Show them what you have!

Over-Fifty Candidates

The US Bureau of Labor Statistics estimates that the number of individuals fifty-five and over has grown by 12 percent over the last decade. As a result of this growth, many issues are developing that need attention. Potential employers may have a great deal of experience and background to consider when evaluating your work history, work ethic, loyalty, and ability to work with other people.

Maybe you're retired from a previous career. You served in the Armed Forces for twenty, twenty-five, thirty or more years. You retired from the New York City Fire Department, and you are now settling in on a second career. All of this works in your favor as a viable candidate. Previous retirement makes you free of other obligations. Usually at this age you're free of the obligations younger people have. You have no children at home, less responsibility, more flexibility, more eagerness, and all of the other advantages found in this fifty-plus age group.

You are a more settled job candidate and may be less likely to have feelings of entitlement. You may be inclined to have less-naïve expectations about a job. Actually, you may have a sense of appreciation that you were given a job at all, especially if you had previously been laid off.

ASSOCIATIONS AND INTERESTS

This section is optional, but it can be an asset, especially when you're limited on experience or are transitioning from one career to another. Your associations and interests can bridge the gap between the two. These include organizations that you have volunteered for and those within the specific industry in which you are applying to work. This section must contribute to an appearance of reliability and support. It needs to enhance your application.

Another way to use this section is to include areas of interest matching the interests of the people you are interviewing with or the company leadership. This section then becomes something you can speak to and create conversations that build rapport.

THE CURRICULUM VITAE

Now it's time to concentrate on your *big guns*. The curriculum vitae or CV is a thorough biographical or autobiographical account of all the education, experience, and background that we keep talking about. It will emphasize all of your professional accomplishments, professional qualifications, and professional activities—no matter what level you are at in the job market.

Curriculum vitae at one time were typically used only in higher-education job situations and often by retired military personnel. CVs have, however, become more and more important in other employment situations. Does that mean it's more important to work up a CV than a résumé? No—when you organize your résumé properly the importance is paramount. If it is written with clarity, skill, and completeness, it will open many doors.

Therefore, you'll want to start off with your résumé. Starting off with your C.V. might be smothering or overwhelming to some potential employers. Use of the CV takes a great deal of poise and self-confidence. It must be used at the proper time. Holding the CV back until the proper moment will increase your chances of selection tremendously.

The CV is a very forceful, motivating, and encouraging way to present yourself to a potential employer. As a specialized instrument, it gives a complete description of your work history. The CV shows in detail any research projects, speeches, seminars, special presentations, and/or publications you took part in, developed, or are working on at this time. It will show any special work details or assignments you have completed or successfully accomplished in your job history.

It may show any special skills you have gained while working in a position. You will also show the carry-over value these skills have and how they prepared you for the job for which you are applying. Your CV is also a great place to describe your volunteer positions and your positions of influence in detail.

In both your résumé and CV, you will, of course, include your name, telephone number where you can be reached, and e-mail address. By law, you no longer have to include age, sex, race, marital status, or other personal data like height and weight.

Be certain to consider the significance of each item listed in the résumé or CV. If an item is not significant to the present job situation, it is best not to use it. Items like hobbies, volunteer activities, ability to speak a foreign language, and various memberships may give a clearer description of qualifications. Again, be especially certain there is a significant reason you are using the items, otherwise they may become nothing more than clutter.

Now that the résumé and CV are imbedded in your mind, let's move on to contact letters—or, more importantly, *motivating letters*.

LETTER WRITING

There are many different types of letter you'll have to write as a job-seeker. You'll start with a motivating letter and move on to a contact letter. Sometimes, sadly, you'll have to write a negative-response letter or no-reply letter; with luck, you'll have an opportunity to write a thank-you letter. This chapter offers more detail on all that writing you'll be doing.

MOTIVATING LETTERS

In a way, every letter should be a motivating letter. Making contact with a potential employer, as I have so often mentioned, is crucial in the job-seeking process. It's a time when you must present yourself in the best light possible. It is again the time when you make that good first impression.

You must show that you have exactly what it takes to satisfy the requirements of the position. No one else can do it but you. You must make such a good first impression that you are the one employers want to hire. You must persuade, influence, stimulate, inspire, move, encourage, arouse, prompt, induce, cause, spur, impel, the potential employer to want you and only you.

In other words, you must motivate the potential employer. For all these reasons, we call this initial letter a motivating letter. This motivating letter must meet a number of basic, standard criteria:

> » It must be mechanically and grammatically acceptable.

> » It should be addressed to an individual at the company or organization. Avoid the impersonal "Dear Sir or Madam." Find out the name of the person and his or her position before writing.

> » It should be no longer than one page.

> » It should describe you, sell you, and show all your favorable points to the potential employer.

> » It should use the personal pronoun *I* as little as possible. As a general rule, no more than one *I* per paragraph.

» It should contain positive descriptions of your qualifications and accomplishments to stimulate the potential employer to look further into your background and learn more about you.

In the initial paragraph, you may be writing in response to an advertised position or a recommended position, or simply writing to inquire about a possible position. The first paragraph of your motivating letter should be directed specifically at the potential employer or the person responsible for the job. You should tell this potential employer just why you are interested in this particular position. Be polite, assertive, and specific, but never aggressive, domineering, or arrogant; be honest and convincing, but not pompous.

In the middle portion of your motivating letter, emphasize your accomplishments. Tell the potential employer all of your strong points. Be sure to use positive adjectives or the action words you'll find in Appendix D. Even if you have just graduated or are about to graduate, you are certain to have many experiences and accomplishments that you can describe. If you were president of your senior class or made Eagle Scout, these all go a long way toward presenting a positive picture of yourself. If you took on prominent positions in a service club or your church, these will help in making your accomplishments look good to an employer.

Of course, if you are at the executive level looking for a job, you will have many more accomplishments to show a potential employer. Emphasize the most noteworthy and the most specific to the job you are seeking. Tell the potential employer exactly why you are exceptionally prepared for the position. Use examples related to the job to show why you are the best candidate. As with the initial paragraph, be polite, be assertive, and be specific.

The third and final paragraph of your motivating letter should be personal in nature. Include your education and a brief statement of your professional goals. Although, by law, employers may not ask discriminating questions about age, sex, marital status, race, or religious preference, you may want to include that information if you see fit.

Finish with a positive statement regarding your desire to work with the potential employer. Tell him or her you would be available for a personal interview or to provide further information or clarification. Use action words, be positive, and remember the more specific favorable contacts you make, the more you increase your chances of getting a job.

Contact Letters

Actually, every letter is a contact letter! Commonly, the response to your original motivating letter is a form letter acknowledging your letter. Often the potential employer will include an application for you to fill out and return. Your response should include another contact letter with the application, reinforcing the points in your original motivating letter.

Like motivating letters, contact letters should restate some of your strong characteristics and point out why you are the best person for the job. Again, make direct reference to the job and the situation. Although contact letters typically are sent after the motivating letter, they should always be considered another motivating letter.

In a sense, your first, second, third, and all of your other contact letters should be motivating letters. As I keep repeating, you never get a second chance to make a good first impression, and this in effect is the best example. Whenever you make another contact with a potential employer you must again make a good first impression. It doesn't matter if it is the motivating letter, a contact letter, a response to a negative reply, a thank-you letter, or whatever.

If you keep in mind the points I made about the motivating letter, you will realize that with all letters, you must do the following:

» Make that good first impression.

» Show that you have what it takes to satisfy the requirements of the position.

» Demonstrate that you are the one, the only one! You must make such a good first impression that *you* are the one they want to hire.

» Persuade, influence, stimulate, inspire, move, encourage, arouse, prompt, induce, cause, spur, and impel the potential employer to want you and only you

As mentioned before, a good contact letter must meet the following criteria:

» It must be mechanically and grammatically acceptable.

» It should be addressed to an individual at the company or organization. Avoid the impersonal "Dear Sir or Madam." Find out the name of the person and his or her position before writing.

» It should be no longer than one page.

» It should describe you, sell you, and show all your favorable points to the potential employer.

» It should use the personal pronoun *I* as little as possible. As a general rule, no more than one *I* per paragraph.

» It should contain positive descriptions of your qualifications and accomplishments to stimulate the potential employer to look further into your background and learn more about you.

These are all of the points mentioned for writing a motivating letter. In no way would you differ in writing a contact letter.

Negative-Response Letters

Regrettably, a common answer to your motivating letter is a negative letter. This letter may state a number of things, but you must respond with another response and another motivating contact letter. You may feel disappointed, but when a reply to a negative letter is used properly, it can open many doors.

As you have done before, be polite, be assertive, and be specific. In a follow-up to a negative reply, you should thank the potential employer for the consideration given and express your disappointment. Ask the potential employer if he or she knows of any other situations that would be appropriate for your unique talents and qualifications. Include another résumé and ask that it be passed along.

No-Reply Letters

Unfortunately, the most common reply to your motivating letter will be no reply. Nothing irritates me more than no reply! But with the cost of postage, the time needed for answering each letter, and the huge number of replies to some job offerings, this is becoming more and more common.

If you feel you're really interested in the job, wait a reasonable amount of time and reply. This reply should inquire about your letter of application, confirm your continuing interest in the job, and restate your particular qualifications. If after all of this time there is no reply to your previous letters, forget about it—you probably wouldn't want to work for that employer in the first place.

Thank-You Letters

A well-prepared, motivating contact letter, regardless of the type, will eventually require a thank-you letter. These go a long way in supporting your applications or qualifications. A thank-your letter is just another polite way of making another good first impression.

Thank-you letters should be sent after every interview, after every negative reply, and even after no reply. Again, be polite, assertive, and concise. Even if a thank-you letter is to a no-reply letter you should still be polite and assertive. Simply make reference to the particular job by asking a question. It can be something very simple, but a question usually elicits a response and an answer to your question and guess what, that may open another door.

The Letter You've Been Waiting For

For those of you who have done your homework and have followed the procedures above, the next letter you receive should be a job offer. Hallelujah! All of your hard work has paid off.

Now what do you do? Take a walk around the block, take a friend to dinner, and celebrate in some appropriate manner?

No, no, and no! Immediately acknowledge receipt of the offer letter. State your appreciation, even though you were the best person for the job and the employer made the best choice possible. Initiate a discussion of when you will start work, and once the starting date is decided, be certain to hold firmly to that date.

Then make arrangements to sign your contract. If for any reason at all you should decide to decline an offer of employment, do so as politely and thoughtfully as possible. You never know when you may be associated with that employer again!

PART III

Social Media

Does social media matter? We hear this question from our clients all the time. In a word—*yes!* Social Media has become so prominent in our society today one can hardly get away without some exposure. Although it has some bad points with its constant exposure it too can be utilized to your advantage.

While it would be nice to think that things will get back to "normal" or the way they "used to be," that is simply not going to happen. Like it or not, the job-seeking world has changed. Organizations large and small, public and private use social media to cut through the unqualified and risky candidates. It saves them time and money to do this research up front. Sometimes, once the list is cut to the top ten or twenty candidates, employers actually hire research firms to do these prescreening background checks. Other organizations do the research themselves.

When you think about it, it makes complete sense. Let's say that an initial interview, even if it's on the phone, costs the organization at least the staff time of the interviewers. If employers can reduce the pool from ten to seven by having a staff member spend an hour or two researching the top dozen candidates, why wouldn't they? Every name cut out potentially saves hundreds of dollars.

The point is that before you submit your résumé or motivating letter, you need to have a complete and up-to-date profile that matches your foundational résumé information. This is now business as usual. In order to gain the competitive advantage, you need to get with the times.

YOUR LINKEDIN PROFILE

LinkedIn is the oldest job and professional social-media site. It boasts a membership of more than 100,000,000—yes, that's 100 million—professionals. While not as large as Facebook, with nearly 600 million active users, LinkedIn is geared toward the professional and business world. Setting up your profile for maximum exposure helps to give you credibility as someone who understands that times have changed. That's a good thing for a potential employer to know.

While we will briefly touch on your profile, if you want to get a systematic, step-by-step guide to setting up and making your LinkedIn profile the very best that it can be, purchase a copy of *Professional Secrets to a Powerful LinkedIn Profile*, available on Amazon.com. This guide also includes how to effectively use LinkedIn to network, how to strategically use LinkedIn groups, and how to showcase your talents while building a good online reputation.

With that said, let's jump into your LinkedIn profile and the delicate balance you as a job-seeker need to maintain.

By now, you're getting the idea that one of the keys to successful job-seeking is successful marketing. You want to be found and stake your claim for who you are and what you do. When you're applying for a job, what does your LinkedIn profile say or not say? Even worse, what if it can't be found?

A recent survey of job-search firms and corporate hiring specialists revealed that more than half (54 percent) of them search for and assess job candidates online before they decide to interview them.

Stop and read that again. They search for you after you apply and before they reach out to you. You need to have your web presence ready for review before you ever submit an application.

Wouldn't it be nice to have a recruiter *find* you through your LinkedIn profile because you are a perfect candidate for a position that he or she has open? Your LinkedIn profile is a 24/7 opportunity to interest a potential employer or recruiter in you, your experience, and how you solve people's challenges.

PROFILE TIPS

Your LinkedIn profile needs to be complete, including a current photo of yourself. A nice headshot is preferable. It can be taken with a regular camera or even a cell-phone camera. Just make sure that the photo is clear, well-lit, and includes just you. Your profile photo is not the place for your pets, spouse, partner, or favorite sports-team logo. This is another "first impression" opportunity. Keep it professional, make it specific, and fit it to the people you want to be working with and the companies you would like to have hired you.

Your "professional headline" is the first thing after your photo and name that visitors will see. This headline will either capture their attention or let them know they can move on to the next person. Just like the personal objective on your résumé, it is critical for this headline to contain the correct keywords so you are associated with the positions that you are seeking.

One important point: everything you write is about and for your profile visitors and how you can help them. Think of it as if you were in their chair reading about a potential job candidate. Remember, they are thinking, "What's in it for me?"

Your LinkedIn summary is the next section, and it's broken down into two parts: professional experience and specialties. Spell out how you benefit people—think of this as your offer—and then list your specialties. This is also a big area for keyword phrases.

The professional experience section is where your résumé ends up after you upload it. Make sure to review this section to make sure that it covers all of your primary skills. Provide some detail, but not so much that you exclude yourself from some of the positions you may be seeking. This is especially true when you're transitioning from one career to another. You may need to review and tweak your profile to emphasize the skills you want to showcase in your new chosen industry and deemphasize your other skills and experiences.

Think of your LinkedIn profile as an umbrella that covers your experience history. It can bring out the specific experiences and knowledge that make you attractive to the organizations that you are applying to now, even if those were not your primary job responsibilities previously.

A note of caution: remember that every connection you have may receive a message (depending on settings) when you update your profile. If you are currently employed and are shifting to a new field, use caution so as to not alert connections that are with your current employer.

Profile links can be used to give your profile visitors more information about you and the organization you are working with now. You can have up to three links to websites as a part of your LinkedIn profile. These links can be to your personal blog, a company website, or any other site you would like to highlight. A best practice is to create anchor text for your link. In other words, instead of "My Website," make the wording relevant to your industry by using keyword phrases, such as "CPA for Manufacturing Companies." This motivates readers to take action by clicking on your link because it is relevant to their needs.

LinkedIn add-on sections highlight accomplishments, giving you an opportunity to stand out from the other professionals in your field. These accomplishments are segmented in their own area, thereby highlighting them and making them easy to find. There are currently three add-on sections:

- » patents
- » languages
- » publications

These are especially important for the academic and scientific communities, where there is truth in the old axiom "publish or perish." In our ever-increasing multicultural and multilingual world, noting which languages you can read, write, and speak is a plus that distinguishes you from others in your area of expertise.

That covers your LinkedIn profile and gives you some good direction on how to get the most from it. Now that you have your LinkedIn profile set up, let's move on to your overall online image.

YOUR ONLINE IMAGE

As mentioned earlier, most employers are now doing background research on all job candidates before they ever respond to the applications they receive. So your Facebook (or Myspace, if you are that old or that counterculture) profile or those blog-post rants that you made while you were ticked off at your then-employer may not help you make that good first impression.

So what do you do?

Well, there are a number of things you can do. Have others help you, and when all else fails, at least be aware of what's out there. You need to be smart with what you post and say online. The downsides are just not worth any possible upsides.

Let's see what you can do to find out what you look like to the rest of the world. If you wanted to do research on something, where would you go? What would you do? Chances are, you'd start with a simple Google search of your name. You can then follow that up with the same search on Bing, Yahoo, and then within Facebook, LinkedIn, and Twitter. You are looking for what anyone else can see about you. Is it what you want them to see?

Maybe more importantly, is it what you want your prospective employer to see? If not, then you have some cleanup to do. First, make a list of the website address (URL) of each page that you would like to not be part of your global profile. If there is more than a page or two that you would like to disappear, I would use a spreadsheet to track them. Label a column for the date found, the URL, the site name, the webmaster or page owner, the contact date, and a column for the result. This simple spreadsheet will help you track your results.

FACEBOOK

Facebook is the largest social network on the planet. It gets billions and billions of page views every day. When assessing your Facebook wall and profile, keep in mind that your employer will be doing the same. In addition to cleaning up the obvious photos and comments on your wall, you also may have been "tagged" in other, shall we say, less than flattering photos by other people. Most of the time, these are well-meaning friends who are joking around or reliving memories of years gone by. In any case, there are a number of things you can do to try to get your tags cleaned up.

» *Remove the image or post from your profile.* Your wall and profile represents you, and you have control over it. Simply remove the things you don't want to show up. By the way, you can also update your privacy settings to prevent automatic postings to your profile.

» *Remove the tag.* You can easily remove the tag from the post. The post will still be on Facebook, but it will no longer link to your profile.

» *Ask the post owner to remove the message.* Sometimes the easiest thing to do is just ask. Again, most of the times they meant no harm in posting that '90s photo with the spiked Mohawk. Just nicely asking the person to remove the post from Facebook works most of the time.

» *Report a post to Facebook.* If the post can be considered abusive, report it to Facebook and it will be removed. This is not the most friendly way to deal with the post, but it can be done.

» *Block the owner of the post.* This is another drastic step, but this will remove all tags from this person and you will no longer be able to see or interact with each other on Facebook.

Looking for a job can be a disheartening experience, and the longer you look, the more discouraged you become. This is a normal feeling, and it is one that you must overcome to get the offer that you are seeking.

You may feel that you are the perfect fit for a position. You meet and even exceed the basic and preferred requirements shown in the position announcement. Yet you don't get even a call for an interview. It's frustrating. Trust me, I know. I have been there and really don't like it very much. The key is to not let this feeling get in your way. You are your best representative and as such you need to present the confidence and belief in yourself that your future employer wants to contact, see, interview, and eventually hire.

OTHER OPTIONS

You may have all of the assets employers are looking for, but you need to know where to find a job before you can show them your stuff. The main thing is to not give up hope. As you will see, there are more options for finding jobs today than ever before.

Newspapers

Newspapers used to be the go-to place for job-seekers. It may be fast and easy to check the want ads, but it has its limitations. Only some of the available jobs in a given area will be published in the paper, so you won't have as many job opportunities as you could by expanding your search.

Newspapers are partnering with online services like CareerBuilder to list local jobs on their websites as well. This shows that papers are trying to stay in the game that used to help pay their bills. Overall, the newspaper—printed or online—is becoming less and less of a player when you are trying to locate a new job or expand your career options.

Job-Search Websites

Job websites can help, but you will be limiting yourself to only those jobs that employers post online. One of the benefits of such sites, however, is that you can quickly find employment opportunities across the globe or right around the corner. We have all heard of the major players in this area: CareerBuilder.com, Monster.com, Craigslist.com, and the higher quality The Ladders.com. There are dozens of other places you can use to search for positions and post your contact or résumé information.

Posting your résumé on these sites, especially in response to job openings, is not a bad thing at all. First, your résumé may be seen by a person looking to fill the position. Second, your profile will be seen by agency recruiters who are looking for talent to place in either full-time or contract positions. However, applying for positions in this way exclusively is invoking the "hope and pray" strategy we discussed earlier. You cannot count on this passive method to get you placed quickly.

More LinkedIn

You are looking for a career in a specific industry, so why not search LinkedIn to find the companies that make up that industry? Then, when you find a good candidate company, search for it and its employees while you are there. You will be surprised at how much you can find out about a company, its products, who it hires, and what other professionals say about it, all on LinkedIn. And with more than 900,000 groups, many of them industry-specific, there are few better places to discover companies that may be looking to hire someone like you.

LinkedIn has a huge collection of professionals who have self-indicated their interests. What do you think are the chances that even small companies have some of their owners and employees listed? Find out by using the advanced search features of LinkedIn. Want to know about the information technology and services industries in Iowa? Search those fields using "Iowa" as a keyword. Or maybe you have a particular skill set you'd like to use in your next job. Use LinkedIn to find out where others with the same skills are working and what their titles are.

Think of the opportunity to open doors to industries that may not have occurred to you. You can research the primary skill sets of the total LinkedIn membership, find out where that skill set ranks within the LinkedIn community, and see related skill sets. Plus, you can find the leading professionals and companies for those particular skills. Once you know who these industry leaders are, you are one step closer to finding them or finding someone you know who knows them. Now that is exciting networking!

Employment Agencies

Most cities and towns of any size will have one employment agency or more. This could be a government-supported center, a temporary-work agency, or one that specializes in corporate positions. Check under "employment agency" in your local phone book to see what services are available in your area.

Organization Websites

If you have a specific organization in mind that you would like to work for, many of them will list openings on their websites. This is a great place to discover job openings because the listings are generally up-to-date and can give more detail than an advertisement would. You may also be able to determine the job classification (and therefore the typical pay range) based on what information is shared or how it is phrased.

Word of Mouth

When it comes to where to find a job, word of mouth or networking is by far the best way to go. More and more organizations are hiring based on internal recommendation. If you know someone who works where there is a position that interests you, talk to him or her about it. If you do not know anyone, use your LinkedIn network to get introduced to someone who does know. This connection will help you get more information about the organization and give you that all-important inside reference.

If you do not have a target organization, letting your network know what you are looking for in the way of a job may uncover one for you. When you strategically let people know that you are looking for a position and what you'd like to do, you are putting the resources of many people to work for you. Now it is not just about all of the places you can find, it's about all of the places that can find you.

Once we had a client who was invited to a cocktail party. It was quite crowded, and while the host and our client were catching up on their lives, the topic of work came up. Their conversation was soon joined by a friend of the host's wife. She had been looking for someone to do exactly what our client was doing for a current client, so they traded contact information. He has done multiple jobs for her company over the years that have passed since that party. Our client would have never known the work even existed and would have been almost $100,000 poorer if he had not talked with his network.

NETWORKING

This brings us to one of the single most powerful job-procurement strategies: networking. We actually network all the time without knowing it, and I will allude to this strategy throughout this book. Networking is about making connections and developing mutually beneficial relationships. It functions as another method for meeting people. Plus, it helps you increase your contacts and widen your scope of influence.

Ultimately, it's not about who you know—it's about who knows you. Personal relationships through networking help you stand out, rise above the rest, and remain on top. Networking will provide you with a very valuable, competent, and lasting method of building relationships. Your success depends on constantly connecting with people, promoting relationships, and facilitating win-win situations. This couldn't be truer than when it comes to job-seeking skills.

Networking really means making yourself known. A very good idea is to have personal business cards printed. Show your full name, your e-mail address, and your telephone numbers. Make it very simple and neat. You do not need your address. Never clutter your business card with more than this necessary information: name, e-mail address, telephone. Nothing more.

Now, when you go to a meeting or business social, you have personal business cards to give out. Use them, and use them frequently. It's only to your benefit! Now let's get a bit more specific on networking and finding positions.

OPEN CALLING AND ADVICE CALLING

There are two other job-seeking skills worth discussing at this point. With these skills especially, you definitely must remember that politeness goes a long way. These job-seeking skills are *open calling* and *advice calling*. Even though they are nontraditional methods of job hunting and may be quite different in many ways, they do require the same type of courteousness, politeness, and assertiveness.

Open Calling

Open calling occurs when you take the lead and call the company manager for the position yourself. It has the possibility of opening many doors, and for this reason alone it is quite effective.

Most recruiting specialists actually utilize these techniques themselves to find jobs in various companies and fields for their clients. There is no reason, however, that you yourself cannot do the open calling instead of hiring a recruiting specialist. In fact, it looks much better if you do the calling yourself. It shows a great deal of assertiveness, determination, and confidence.

According to a great deal of scientific research, open calling works better than traditional job-seeking methods. That does not mean, however, that you will not need your résumé, profile, motivating letter, or other contact letters. It only means you may use them at a different time and in a different way.

You will also use the same fact-finding techniques mentioned earlier for finding out information about the company. With this information in hand, you personally will call the manager or the person in charge of the job directly.

Be polite and assertive. Ask for a minute of his or her time. Be brief and be concise. Express your interest in the particular job. Ask if you may send your résumé directly to this individual for consideration.

The manager, at that time, may ask you a few questions. Answer to the best of your knowledge and conclude with any questions of your own. If you did your homework completely, you will have something to say.

More likely than not, managers seek to have control over the people who work for them. They know if they select a candidate from among those they interview, more than likely they will choose the right person.

Candidates for a particular job who have the motivation, determination, and confidence to contact the manager on their own are in a much better position for selection. When managers themselves recommend a candidate to personnel or human resources for a job, it carries much more weight than anything else. This is the person who is hired.

Advice Calling

Advice calling is the best type of skill you can possibly develop. It can be used continuously throughout your career and it can enhance you in many ways, but it is also the most difficult job-seeking skill to develop and use. Advice calling takes a great deal of determination, purpose, willpower, and just plain resourcefulness. It really is the ultimate in job-seeking skills.

Whether you are just out of college, a middle manager, or perhaps even a top-level executive, you'll find that this technique works perfectly at each level and in each instance. For example, if there is a particular field you are trained or educated in, or you want to work in, or you already work in, select a company and field in which you have an interest. Go to the Internet and do your homework. Find out the name of the president, CEO, or even executive vice president. Find out all you possibly can about that person: where from, schools attended, publications, and even recreational interests.

Now, make a direct call to this president, CEO, or whomever you choose and explain your situation. Tell him or her that you're just out of college, you've just completed your MBA, you're considering a career change, or you're trying to decide on an upper-level executive move. Be very frank, candid, and sincere. Say you selected him or her because you value his or her position and the advice he or she may be able to give you in this situation. Emphasize the fact you are not looking for a job, you are only looking for advice, and you will only take a short amount of time.

When this individual or his or her secretary sets up an appointment, you will then follow all of the steps you will learn later in the book about interview skills. Know the exact time, date, and place; arrive at least fifteen minutes early for the appointment; be certain to make a good first impression. Even though you may be nervous, try to appear calm. Be polite, cordial, and relaxed.

If the person you're talking to takes the lead, go with it! You may have an inclination to be assertive, but let that occur naturally. You might interject the condition of the economy, but do not ever get into a discussion of politics, religion, or sex. Remember, you can never win this discussion, and under these circumstances it definitely is not advisable.

You may be asked, "How can I help you?" If not, be sure to state the real reason you are there: *for advice.* You have just graduated from college, or you are considering a career change, or you are considering an executive move. You value the opinion of someone with his or her particular education, experience, and background.

At that point, take the lead and go from there. I once had a client who went on an advice call to the president of a subsidiary company of a parent group. This president felt certain he had no openings for our client. He suggested, however, "Maybe the vice president of development in our parent group could use you."

What do you think happens when presidents of a subsidiary company calls vice presidents of marketing or directors of human resources for the parent group? They get results!

In this case, the president of the subsidiary company did pick up the phone and call the vice president of marketing for the parent group. Guess what happened next? An interview was set up immediately.

As a result of this advice call, our client met the vice president of marketing and got an interview with a manager working directly under the vice president. The manager was more than happy to interview our client. Sure enough, our client got the job. What a pleasant surprise!

This may be the best job-seeking skill you can use, but it may be the most difficult. You must put away any fears and worries and always keep in mind this job-seeking skill is the best. Despite the fact that the "fear factor" keeps most people away from open calling and advice calling, they are still the best, and they do work very effectively.

Why Open Calling and Advice Calling Works

There are a number of reasons we feel that open calling and advice calling will help you in finding a job:

» They put you directly in contact with the person who is the key player in the company's hiring process. Remember, 95 percent of most résumés never get any consideration because they are never read. Using open calls or advice calls improves your chances' tremendously because you eliminate the initial screening which does nothing more than simply miss good candidates like yourself.

» These calls are often taken out of courtesy or curiosity. Keep in mind that an open call or advice call is very difficult to refuse if you are well-informed, courteous, polite, and assertive. All you need is a few minutes of time. If you are fully prepared to make a strong case for yourself in a short period of time, most managers will give you a few minutes.

» In many instances, the best jobs are not posted or advertised. A well-placed open call or advice call may put you in a position to locate or uncover these jobs. Think of the tremendous advantage this gives you, in view of the fact that a good number of jobs are filled from inside knowledge or even before they are posted.

» Many hiring positions are created by managers on the spur of the moment. These managers have someone in mind long before they may be ready to hire. Sometimes, especially in the higher-executive-level positions, the person is found through their own resources. Why not be one who shows personal initiative with an open call or advice call and doesn't simply rely on a résumé or other source?

» Often the most important result of an open call or advice call is that it provides referrals from the first company to another company that may be hiring. These contacts can point you in the right direction and open doors that were previously locked. The referral often acts as a recommendation from one to the other, which is another positive in you favor.

» If you have done your homework, when you open call or advice call, you are the one who can govern the way in which you present information. This allows you to play to your strong points and present yourself in the best light possible. You are now in a position to call attention to facts showing you are the best candidate possible.

» When you make an open call or an advice call, you gain more and more experience with each call. You'll become better and better at selling your strong points. You'll be successful because you become aware of more and more jobs that aren't advertised or publicized.

» By utilizing an open call or an advice call, you place yourself in a better position to be remembered by the manager. You were the individual who took the initiative to make an effort, either by telephone or in person, to talk with the manager or president personally. All other candidates only relied on a résumé to show off their abilities for the job.

» If you plan on changing careers, an open call or advice call is always the most effective. Oftentimes you will have difficulty showing on a résumé how you can move from one area to another. Using an open call or an advice call gives you an opportunity to emphasize strong points in person. You would not be able to begin to show these on a résumé. This is what shows your versatility for movement into a different area or career.

In each of these examples, when using an open call or advice call, keep in mind that you *must* have a follow-up. Regardless of the outcome of these calls, you must respond with a follow-up letter. Whether it is a thank-you letter, a letter asking another question, or whatever, use the opportunity to make another good first impression, regardless of where you are in the employment process.

PART IV

Interviewing Skills

This is where all of your hard work comes to fruition and you're really going to find out what you're really made of. This is where the "make or break" part of the job-seeking process takes place. Here you will have an opportunity to shine, and you certainly do not want to do less than your best.

Up to this point, you must have made a good first impression with this potential employer, or you would not be having this interview. Your initial contacts must have gotten their attention, so *The Expert's Job-Seeking Methods* are working. Let's keep moving forward.

Again, you obviously want to present yourself in the best light possible. This means you want to appear to be knowledgeable, interested, concerned, confident, able, and dedicated. For each interview, you will want to complete your pre-interview research. This research builds on the background investigation that you have already completed, so you are more than halfway there.

ASSERTIVE VS. AGGRESSIVE

Throughout this book, I have tried to convey a philosophy of respect, consideration, thoughtfulness, sensitivity, and understanding—not only from the standpoint of the job-seeker, but also from that of the perspective employer and perhaps your total personality and method of operation.

This may be an altruistic approach to job-seeking, but in the long run, I feel it is the better approach. Ultimately, it pays off, not only if you get the job and succeed but also if you do not get the job and need to go on looking. Eventually, it will result in a win-win situation.

Before you actually contact your prospective employers, you'll need to do some research on how to create this win-win solution. While it often happens as a result of being assertive, many people confuse assertiveness with aggressiveness. *Assertive* and *aggressive*, however, are two very different types of communication behavior:

» *Assertive* describes a confident personality that maintains consideration of others.

» *Aggressive* describes a selfish personality focused on pursuing one's own goals and interests forcefully and sometimes excessively.

When you are assertive, you communicate clearly and with confidence. You are able to express your needs, desires, or wishes confidently while also respecting the needs, desires, or wishes of others. Aggressive people, in contrast, respond to the uncertainty, selfishness, and disrespect of others. It shows a general *lack* of confidence. Aggression will make you appear to be a very self-serving person in pursuit of your own desires or wishes.

Please note the keyword in both definitions is *confidence*. You must be confident to be assertive, but you will appear to lack confidence when you are aggressive. That's not to say you *can't* be confident while being aggressive, but usually aggressiveness is a response to uncertainty. If you are not certain of something, you cannot be confident.

Being assertive is a basic communication skill. When you are assertive, you express yourself effectively and confidently, while at the same time respecting the rights and beliefs of others. Being assertive also helps you to increase and maintain your self-esteem. As you know, your self-esteem goes hand in hand with earning the respect of others and therefore establishing mutual respect.

According to the Mayo Clinic, assertiveness can help you control your stress and anger and improve coping skills. For this reason, you will want to recognize and use assertive behavior in your communications. Learn to be assertive, because it infuses your whole personality. It shows in your letter-writing skills, it comes through over the telephone, and it definitely stands out when you interview.

BODY LANGUAGE SPEAKS VOLUMES

We all know communication isn't just verbal. Your body language is a great example of communication. The way you walk, the way you talk, the way you sit, the way you hold your hands, and the way you make eye contact are all part of nonverbal communication. These behaviors can count a great deal in your communication, especially in your interview.

Walk and act confidently, and keep an upright posture. If possible, make eye contact with each interviewer. Maintain a neutral facial expression, keep your hands still, leave your hair alone, and follow the lead of the interviewer.

I really can't resist telling this story. Once when I was in-house counsel for a large school district, we interviewed numerous individuals for what would eventually be a number of important and rather high-level management positions. A personal friend had recommended one individual for this management position. This person had impeccable credentials, and I personally thought he would fit in extremely well.

Unfortunately, when the recommended individual arrived, he had very poor posture, his head was down, and he never made eye contact. To make matters worse, he sat through the interview with either his arms folded and crossed in front of him or his legs crossed with the ankle at the knee.

Do you think he was even considered for the job? No, no, no! In spite of his impeccable credentials, body language was his downfall. He was not even called back for a second interview. That certainly says something about body language!

Learn to be assertive in writing, speaking, walking, talking, sitting, and carrying yourself by doing the following:

» Walk with you head high and with straight posture.

» Sit comfortably and erect.

» Answer questions completely without rambling.

» Use your hands quietly.

Start thinking and acting this way now. Make it a part of your everyday life, starting today.

BE PREPARED

Y ou have two primary objectives at your initial interview:

1. Provide the organization with enough information to determine whether or not there is mutual interest and a reason to continue with further contact.

2. Get your questions and concerns addressed so that you can make a good decision if you are offered the position.

The interview is actually nothing more than a conversation between two or more people to assess whether a mutually beneficial partnership or association can be formed.

The following interview advice, even though it may contradict many of the so-called experts, will put you at the head of the pack for getting the all-important offer for the position that you have been working toward.

When you are scheduling your interview, it is more than appropriate for you to ask for the names and titles of the people with whom you will be interviewing. This can give you some very valuable information. First, you'll get an idea of how many people you will be interviewing with, and more importantly, the interviewers' names and positions. Make sure you also ask for proper spellings if the names are not common.

Expand Your Research

Remember the process we discussed earlier about researching the organization using information from the Internet, LinkedIn, and various print publications like catalogs, trade journals, and press releases. You'll want to dig a little deeper now as you go into the interviewing process.

Since you have already done the background research on the organization before writing your letters, you should have a good feel for what it does, how it does it, and what kind of culture it has. Is there anything else you want to know about the organization? Start creating a list of questions for your interview.

Since you have the names of your interviewers, you can dig up some information on them as well. Start by searching the organization's website for their profiles, comments they have made, and where they fit in the organizational structure. Then research them on Google, including their bosses. See if you can find LinkedIn profiles not just for your interviewers but for other managers and near-level executives as well. You never know who you will get a chance to meet while onsite.

You are looking for answers to any and all of these questions:

» Where did they graduate from school?

» Where do they live?

» What are their hobbies?

» What associations are they a part of?

» What are they reading?

This type of information allows you to find ways to build rapport with interviewers and anyone else you might meet. It's important to find common ground.

I once had a client who, through his research, found out his interviewer was in the same fraternity at a neighboring college. Casually during the interview, our client mentioned his fraternity, and immediately they became fast friends. The interviewer actually said, "I can say that I have interviewed many candidates for this position, and you can rest assured you will be on top of my list." Do you really think he was that much better than the other candidates, or do you think his fraternity brother was just looking out for him?

Practice Your Responses

Just as with anything else in life, you gain confidence with practice and experience. So practice, practice, practice, and confidence will follow close behind.

The worksheets in the appendix of *The Expert's Job-Seeking Methods* will help you stay organized so that when you get to your interview, you have your thoughts in order. By practicing your responses to the common questions found in Appendix E, whether in your head or (preferably) verbally with someone else, you will have a greater presence about yourself and will be much better prepared.

Practice is applicable to any level of the job applicant. You may be interviewing for an entry-level position, or you may be reaching for a high-level executive position. We all need to practice to be at our very best.

Personal Appearance

Personal appearance *always* plays an important part in making a good first impression. The idea is to match the culture of the organization with which you are interviewing. If the culture of the organization is conservative, then dress conservatively. If the culture is more relaxed, you can get away with being more relaxed. It's always good to play it safe with your appearance until you really know the day-to-day workings of the organization.

However, in an initial interview, it would be advisable to dress in your most conservative outfit. Men should wear a shirt and tie with a suit or sport jacket and conservative slacks. Women should wear a modest dress, or a skirt or slacks with a blouse or sweater. Make sure you are in keeping with accepted business wear.

A judge once told me, "When you appear in court, you can wear any color suit you want, as long as it is dark blue or black; and you can wear any color shoes you want, as long as they are black." In the past, this was sage advice. Today you can sometimes get away with much more in the right organizations. Suits, ties, and "classic professional" dress are no longer the standard, but know your organization before you go too casual.

In addition to your clothing choices, your hair needs to match the culture as well. This will vary depending on the organization. Consider, for example, the difference between a New York City brokerage firm and an upscale fashion organization. Be sure to match your environment.

A FEW DON'TS

While I prefer to focus on the things that you *do* want to do, there are some things that are definite *do nots*. These seem like common sense, but you would not believe how many times interviewees have violated one or more of these rules. While I cannot say that these will kill your chances at getting an offer letter, I can say that I have never made an offer to someone who has broken one of these rules.

» Do not slight or make derogatory remarks about anyone, especially a former or current employer or boss. Even if it was the worst sweatshop in the world, don't do it. Come up with a "creative differences" type answer to the question about that "bad boss" we have all had.

» Do not engage in any discussion about politics, religion, or sex. You are usually wrong! It would always be wise to steer very clear of any conversation regarding these topics—even if the interviewer asks.

» Do not give the interviewer the idea you are looking for other positions or are "job shopping." Even if you are trying to create leverage, this will not help your cause.

» Do not chew gum or have anything in your mouth during the interview. Even if the interviewer offers you something, politely refuse.

» Do not slouch in your chair. Sit up straight. This cannot be overemphasized, so pay close attention.

» Do not—I repeat, *do not*—fold your arms across your chest or cross your legs above the ankles. This goes for men and women both.

» Do not have busy hands. Keep your hands very still. Refrain from running your hands through your hair or touching any parts of your body, including your face and especially your nose, ears, and eyes.

» Do not lose eye contact. Maintain eye contact at all times. If there is more than one interviewer, make eye contact with each one as needed.

» Do not condemn, criticize, or complain about anyone, anything, or anyplace.

Going back to the point about not condemning or criticizing anyone or anything, I once had an interview for a job I really wanted. It was for a very prestigious university, and it would have been a great appointment.

I had just finished my master's degree, and this position was a tenured track for a doctorate. The interview went great! After initial conversation and discussion, they took me to lunch at the faculty dining room. They introduced me to many faculty members as their next professor. At the conclusion, we went back to the department chairman's office. I sat outside as he handled some matters in his office.

His secretary then struck up a very friendly conversation and eventually it got into politics. I was very excited about the last presidential election, and I went a little too far in expressing my political opinion. Low and behold, my comments did not sit well with the secretary or the chairman of the department.

Guess what? I was very quickly dismissed and waited a long time before I heard from them. When the letter finally came, it simply said they were happy to announce that they had chosen Mr. So-and-So as their new tenure-track professor. It was another candidate, not me.

About seven years later, I met the candidate they had chosen at a conference, and we discussed his position. He openly stated that the only reason he got the job was that their first choice made derogatory remarks about the university president's brother during the interview and that simply did not sit well with anyone. Live and learn!

INTERVIEWING TIPS

On a more positive note, here are some of the more successful things you should do during and after an interview:

» Stay on purpose and focused. Small talk may help you relax, but do not stray too far away from the real reason for the interview: getting you the offer.

» Even if it is up to you, keep the interview on track.

» Be very courteous and friendly during the interview but not too informal.

» If you do not know an answer to a question, just say so. Admitting that you don't know the answer is in many cases seen as a positive trait. It means that you are likely to be a team player and are willing to ask for help.

Before You Go

Before you leave your home base for the interview, be sure that you have the following:

» good directions to the interview location

» a full tank of gasoline, if you're driving

» the correct fare, if you're riding in public transportation or a taxi

» your contact's phone number (just in case)

» a pen or other writing implement

» a notepad for taking notes and writing down questions

» your background organization research worksheets

» your list of questions for the interviewers

» a copy of your résumé for each of the interviewers plus one

If you have a lucky charm and it makes you feel good, bring it along. Just make sure you put it away prior to entering the building. Remember, you don't know who is watching or is associated with the organization. Just be cautious. Forewarned is forearmed.

The Arrival

Conventional wisdom says to arrive for your interview early and never ever late. We have to say this is 100 percent right. It is, however, only a good idea to a certain point. Showing up too early can make you appear anxious and conspicuous as you sit waiting for your interview.

Fifteen minutes or so is early enough. This allows you to complete any paperwork necessary for the organization and most importantly, it gives you a chance to take a deep breath or two before you meet your interviewers. You want to be early enough to convey promptness, but not so early that people start thinking, "Who is that person who's been sitting in the lobby all morning?"

Sometimes things that are unavoidable happen as you are traveling to your interview. While being late is not the end of the world, it's also not the best foot to get off on when interviewing. If something does happen, make sure you have the contact phone number for the company so that you can call as soon as you know you will be late. Check to see if it is okay to come in late or if it would be better to reschedule the interview. Be polite and accommodating, as it is not this person's fault that something delayed you.

If you do arrive too early, wait in your car or at a nearby coffee shop—but be careful not to ramp up on caffeine, as you don't want to appear to be hyper during the interview! Target that magic fifteen minutes prior to the scheduled interview start time.

Once you have arrived, check in with the receptionist or your contact person by stating your name, who you are scheduled to meet with, and what time the interview is scheduled to start. This presents you to the first person you meet as confident and collected. Remember, everyone is paying attention to you. Treat everyone with respect and courtesy.

Now is a great opportunity to take a moment and get focused. A trick we use is to be seated and relax. If you are like most people, you will be a little nervous or tense. Here is an opportunity to use a helpful relaxation technique: Slowly inhale deeply, counting to ten. Next, hold your breath for another count of ten. Finally, quietly exhale, counting to ten again. Do this a few times, and you will have actually provided your brain with a good supply of oxygen and slowed your heart rate. As a result, you will be much more relaxed.

During the Interview

All of your previous good first impressions are now going to be put to the test. The interview is the time to really present yourself. It's your interview, so all of the preparation and coaching you have received is over. You are now prepared to ace this interview, so go forward and do your best. The interview is where you really get to express yourself—where you now get to show just how qualified and perfect you are for the job. Remember: be assertive, be positive, and be confident.

When interviewers introduce themselves to you, make sure you get the name and spelling. If possible, ask for a business card. If you have trouble with the interviewer's name, ask him or her to repeat it or spell it for you.

People are generally proud of their name. If it sounds Polish, French, or Scandinavian, for example, ask about it. The person will usually give you some history or a derivation of the name. This helps break the ice and puts you on firmer ground.

When you go into the interview, you may be nervous. I have never personally gone into an interview without being nervous. That is quite natural! In fact, a little nervousness may be helpful.

If the interviewer offers a hand to shake hands, do so—especially if the interviewer is a woman. Make sure it's a firm grip but not too firm. You're definitely not trying to arm wrestle with the interviewer, but an initial handshake does send a message.

On the other hand, do not shake hands like a limp-wristed individual. I cannot even begin to say what message this sends. Wait until the interviewer asks you to sit down and follow from there.

Some quick reminders

» Be pleasant, friendly, cordial, and to the point.

» Answer all questions completely.

» Stay focused and on topic.

» Make eye contact with each interviewer as you answer questions.

» Keep things congenial and relaxed.

WHAT TO EXPECT

Regardless of how much preparation you do, you never really know what the interview is going to be like until it starts. The organization may be interviewing many candidates and then selecting the best candidates for a second round. I once had an interview for a position in which they interviewed all of the candidates at the same time—all together! What an experience!

You can imagine how important it was to obtain as many facts about the situation as possible before that interview. I had to use those facts as best I could in a very brief period of time. During the interview, I suggested they combine areas and departments and retain only one chairman to manage the total area. They used this advice and, unfortunately, retained a person already present within the company. I'm sorry to say my suggestion was utilized but not in my favor and I did not get the job.

Some Typical Questions

There are always the standard questions that interviewers like to put in to see how you will handle them. One of the most often used is a question dealing with your biggest fault or weakness. Many of the experts will tell you to say something like, "I'm a perfectionist," thinking that such a trait will be appealing to an employer. The truth is that the interviewer is waiting for you to give the standard answer, and if you do, it will be just like everyone else's answer. It could even hurt you in the interviewer's mind.

I suggest that you turn the question around in your favor by being honest, but not in a way that relates to your employment. For example, you could say, "I really like to sleep late on Sundays, and I don't always get a good start on my yard work." By doing this, you will show that you are a real person and that you consider laziness a fault. However, you are only saying it happens on Sundays, which is a day of rest for most people anyway.

Questions to Ask

It's your turn now. Ask the questions that you want to ask of the interviewer. Remember this is about a good working relationship for both sides. You need to know the philosophy of the organization. Will it be mutually agreeable? What do people already working there think? What does the environment look like? Where will you be working if you accept the offer that is made? Posturing and strength here will help in the overall process. It shows you believe in yourself and you are not just soliciting.

Providing a good list of questions at this point puts you in a more favorable light. It shows a great deal of initiative on your part. Remember again: be positive, be courteous, and be assertive.

Process Review

We have now taken you through the process of interview skills. Now is the time, after each interview, to sit down and review you thoughts and experiences. Make notes of what you did and what you can think of concerning what you didn't do. Each interview should become easier and easier. Before long, you will be a real expert.

PSYCHOLOGICAL TESTING

Another area it's important to be aware of is psychological testing. This is not intended to make you all psychologists; rather, it is designed to let you know that a good number of organizations use psychological testing to measure personality traits.

These tests can be given prior to the interview, but because there is generally a testing fee the organization must pay to use and score the test, they are usually given after your interview or as a follow-up to your interview. Though such tests are far from perfect, you should be aware of them anyway. Their use is getting to be more and more widespread, and they can throw you for a loop if you're not careful.

Please recognize these psychological tests are not magically, miraculously, or overwhelmingly effective. They simply assess and evaluate information you might give a particular examiner. They are given either in the form of answers to questions by an interviewer or answers on paper in response to specific questions on a test. In the long run, a test's accuracy depends on how honestly and wisely you answered the questions. You will not find any standard professional or psychological tests on the Internet or in a library because they are copyrighted by the test publishers and seldom released for public use.

Psychological tests are also called *psychological assessments*, and they may fall into a number of categories. Each category is designed for a specific purpose and is limited in use. The categories include the following:

» *Achievement and aptitude tests*, usually seen in educational and employment settings, are designed to determine how much you know about a certain topic or how much capacity you have to master materials or skills in a particular area or field.

» *Intelligence tests* measure your intelligence or your ability to comprehend the world around you. They test your ability to take in information and apply its functioning while enhancing the quality of your life. Intelligence is a measure of potential, not a measure of what you have learned. An achievement test is a measure of what you have learned, while an intelligence test is supposed to be culture-free. Most intelligence tests are not culture-free but, in fact, are very culture-biased.

» *Neuropsychological tests* attempt to measure deficits in cognitive functioning—such as your ability to think, speak, reason—that result from some sort of brain damage, such as a stroke or brain injury.

» *Occupational tests* attempt to match your interests with the interests of persons in known careers. The logic here is if the things that interest you in life match up with the things that interest someone in a particular career, you might be successful in that career.

» *Personality tests* are designed to measure your basic personality style. Sometimes called *personality traits* or *leadership style* reports, they are used in clinical or medical settings to help with diagnosis, and in a business setting to assess how you will fit in with the existing environment. Three of the best-known personality tests are the Myers-Briggs, MMPI, and Rorschach test.

» *Specific clinical tests* attempt to measure specific matters, such as your current level of anxiety or depression.

Psychological tests were designed for three main reasons, which are interrelated:

1. It is easier to get information from tests than from clinical interviews.

2. The information from tests is more scientifically consistent than the information from clinical interviews.

3. It is harder to get away with lying on a psychological test than in a clinical interview.

One major problem with psychological tests is their ability to measure what they are intended to measure. This measure of accuracy or usefulness of a test is known as *validity*. Another major problem is the tests' ability to give consistent results over and over again. This measure of consistency is known as *reliability*.

The important thing to remember when constructing or administering any test is that without reliability, there will be no validity. If the test does not consistently measure what it purports to measure, then the test is invalid.

You must also recognize that no psychological test is ever completely valid or reliable. The human mentality or personality is just too complicated to test with full certainty. That's the main reason there can be such uncertainty about some cases even after extensive testing.

Under the proper circumstances and conditions, psychological testing can be very useful—for example, when the various restraints created by psychological testing are properly known, valued, and used in their correct perspective. Unfortunately, the reverse is often the case: psychological testing is not properly used and does not particularly measure what it purports to measure, and it therefore is not consistent in its measurement. In other words, it has a low validity and a low reliability, or no validity or reliability at all.

Every score you receive on a psychological test is nothing more than the score you have gotten on that particular test, at that particular time, and on that particular day. Another test or even the same test given at another time on another day may indeed find completely different results. So what are we saying about psychological testing?

» It may not be very reliable. For this reason, you may test differently from day to day.

» It may not be very valid. You could be tested on material that has nothing to do with your ability to do the job.

» It is difficult to beat. You would have a hard time showing anything but your true traits, aptitude, or knowledge because of the overlapping of questions and the variations of questions.

If you are being given a psychological test, you have rights as a consumer to know the answers to the following questions:

- » Why am I being given the test?

- » What are the names of the test being given?

- » What were the results of the test, including any psychological reports?

- » Who will have access to the test results? Even though you may have signed a release form, it does not mean that everyone can have access to your information.

A friend of mine finished his master's degree and took a direct commission as a second lieutenant in the United States Army. His master's degree was in psychology with an emphasis on psychological testing. In one particular psychometrics course, he studied all of the various psychological tests. One of these was the Wechsler Test, which has a comprehensive part and a perceptual part. He was in a group that worked specifically on the perceptual part of the Wechsler Test.

During his tour of duty, he was injured in the line of duty and suffered a severe cerebral concussion. In fact, he was unconscious for about ten days. When he was ready to be discharged from the army, he stated on his release papers that he was injured in the line of duty and he intended to file for compensation against the US government.

The army immediately sent him to Walter Reed hospital for medical review. When it came time for the psychological testing, what did they give him? You guessed it—the perceptual part of the Wechsler Test.

Needless to say, he did just great! He aced it, you might say. He had all of the medical personnel confused. How could he have brain damage and do so well on this psychological test? Eventually he told them his background and they gave him another test, but he sure had them confused for a time. Psychological testing in some cases can be very confusing.

Now you've had a brief overview on psychological testing. You may not like it and you may find it to be quite annoying, but it is a fact of job-searching today. It is the current craze, and you must accept it.

THE SECOND INTERVIEW

When you get through the first interview with flying colors, the potential employer may call you in for a second interview. Sometimes there may be a third or fourth. In each instance, handle the interview in a similar way as the first. Prepare yourself in the same manner. Expect to meet other people. Use what you've learned about the principle of good first impressions. Use this often.

The Offer

A sweet-sounding word! When the offer is made, arrange to meet with your employer. Make all arrangements for signing a contract, salary and benefits, position and starting date. Look forward to having a job and rest confident in accomplishing a major milestone in your lifetime.

CONCLUSIONS AND COMPLETIONS

I've shown you many of the skills you need to apply for jobs and go on interviews. By no means, however, are these skills and techniques written in stone.

The most important thing is to always make a good first impression—whether it is in your résumé, your motivating letters, your follow-up letters, or your interviews. Remember, you never get a second or a third or a fourth chance to make a good first impression!

In fact this is only the start of our effort to help you and many others find jobs in our turbulent times. No doubt as we broaden our already extensive experiences and contacts we will be broadening our skills in helping you find a job or advancing your position.

It has been a pleasure working with you and helping you on this journey. Like everything in life, there is always room for more improvement and more information.

If you have questions or suggestions regarding this guidebook or the content it contains, please feel free to contact me through my website at www.jobseekingskills.com, where you can also find further information and clarification.

N.B.: Additional information may be obtained by attending one of my Job Seeking Seminars. These seminars are held in various parts of the USA throughout the year. In session one, I spend approximately two to three hours lecturing completely on the materials covered in my manual. All aspects of the manual are covered with emphasis on individual attention to job seeking skills. In session two I spend two to three more hours working with you to aid in development of your own personal job seeking skills. None of my groups are more than 40 participants in size so that each individual gets the personal attention they need

My specially arranged consultations can also be scheduled and spent working individually with you on a one-to-one basis in development of skills for your total personal job seeking package.

Check with my website at www.jobseekingskills.com for further information and clarification

APPENDIX A

Résumés and Profiles

Résumé Example 1–Recent College Graduate, Accounting Position, No Work Experience

John J. Jones
1234 Any street
Anytown, USA 01234

555-555-5555
jjones@swich.co

System Accounting and Programming

Extremely professional and relatively new college graduate with a reputation for quality, efficiency, and diligence verifiable by both employers' and professors' satisfaction and praise. Strengths include:

» **Statistical Analysis and Referencing**

» **Analytical Accounting and Programming**

» **Analytical Reasoning and Design**

» **System Accounting and Leadership**

"John J. Jones has been one of the most delightful and eager students I have worked with in my college teaching career. He is self-motivated, very reliable, and extremely enthusiastic. His competence will be an asset to any company that hires him."—Professor Howard D. Trumble, Chair of Accounting Department and Director of Accounting Certification Board, University of Anystate

Education

Bachelor of Science in Statistical Accounting and Programming—2011
University of Anystate, City, State

Completed all required courses for my degree, including Statistics Research and Design, Analytical Statistics and Reasoning, Reference Accounting and Predictability, Motivational and Psychological Leadership, and Analysis and Design of Accounting Layouts. Graduated Magna Cum Laude.

Computer Skills

Microsoft Word, Microsoft Office, Excel, Fortran, STS,
Windows, Word, Web Design, MS Office.

Experience

Personal/Accounting Assistant
My Computer Advisor   City, State   2006-2011
>> Assistant to Store Manager

>> Provided Statistical Analysis for Programming

Professional Student Advisor   City, State   2004-2006
>> Assisted Students in Learning Computer Skills

>> Developed Programs for Personal Accounting Skills

>> Augmented the Learning of Personal Accounting Programs

Assistant Manager Office Designs   City, State   2002-2004
>> Responsible for Stock Inventory

>> Combined a work schedule with school schedule successfully.

References will be furnished upon request.

Résumé Example 2–Recent College Graduate, Entry Level with BS–MS and Intern Work Experience

Samuel Johnson

Cell-555-555-5555

sjohnson@hos.com

<u>Permanent Address</u>	<u>School Address</u>
456 Central Avenue	123 Main Street
City, State 09753	City, State 09876

<u>Job Objective</u>

» **A highly motivated Architectural Engineer with a track record of improving quality, efficiency, and client satisfaction during previous employment with a concentration on Environmental Design Reinforcement looking for a position in the present field.**

<u>Strengths Presently Include</u>

» Wind and Water Load Calculations

» Reinforced Design for Environmental Protection

» Evaluation of Conditions for ADA Compliance

» Coordination of Final Analysis and Presentation

<u>Education</u>

Central University, City, State
Bachelor of Engineering and Master of
Architectural Engineering (Dual Program)   June 2012

» (Emphasis in Environmental Protection)Completed course work and strengths in Manual and Computer Documentation; Environmental Research and Testing;

ADA Compliance; Environmental Design Reinforcement; Environmental Quality Assurance; Government Agency Regulation.

Experience

The Engineering Associates, Some State   May–August, 2010–2011
» Environmental Engineering Intern

> » Wind and Water Effects on the Environment

> » Structural Design for Improvement of the Environmental

> » Developing ADA Compliance for Evaluations

> » Coordination of Final Printing on Special Environmental Project

Additional Accomplishments
» Designs for Campus Improvement

» Development of ADA Environmental Structures

» Delivery of Structural Proposals in 2009 and 2010

» Directly Involved in Planning and Development of Environmental Cleanup

» First Architectural Engineering Student to Use Computer Analysis in Environmental Design

Volunteer Work

» Boy Scouts of America (Eagle Scout)

» Beautification of City, State Parks

» Landscaping and Design of Special Parks

» Feed the Hungry Program

Certifications

» Passed the Architectural Engineering Exam (certification forthcoming)

» Admitted to the Environmental Development Agency

Affiliations

» Society for Architectural Engineers (president, college section)

» President, Environmental Development and Improvement Society

References will be furnished upon request.

Résumé Example 3—Recent PhD Graduate, Entry Level with Work Experience

John Clark
234 South Street
City, State 34567
JohnC@hotmail.com
456-567-6789

Professional Summary

Highly motivated candidate for doctoral degree in exercise physiology. Successfully completed internships at leading fitness facilities. Seeking position as an exercise physiologist in a developmental or rehabilitative setting.

Strengths Include:

» Development of programs for chronic pulmonary and heart diseases

» Coordinating athletic rehabilitation from injury and surgery

» Facilitation with disabled individuals for daily functioning

» Assisting healthy individuals improve their overall fitness and health for prevention of future disease

Education

University of State   City, State   2012

» Candidate for doctoral degree in Exercise Physiology, May 2012

» Current research: "Effects of Selected Rehabilitation Activities on Knee Injuries"

» Doctoral dissertation: "Relationships of Selected Physiological Fitness Programs Toward the Improvement of Chronic Pulmonary Disease"

» Cumulative GPA: 3.688

» Graduate courses included Advanced Physiology of Exercise, Kinesiology,

Biomechanics, Physiological Psychology, Psychometrics, Research and Design.

City College   City, State   2008

» Master of Science in Biology. Emphasis on Human Anatomy and Physical Therapy. Graduated Magna Cum Laude.

Town College   City, State   2006

» Bachelor of Science in Health and Physical Education

Experience

Physical Fitness Internships (6 weeks—summers of 2006, 2007, 2008, 2009, 2010)

» City, State

» Outpatient Rehabilitation

» Health Care & Fitness Training

» City, State

» Individual Fitness Programs

» Utilization of Equipment

» Organization of Classes

Various Duties

» Development of fitness programs meeting needs of a variety of clients and their problems

» Program evaluation, treatment, and assessment

» Reviewing of information submitted by client's doctor regarding medical condition and therapeutic exercises

» Analysis of the progress of the individual

» Measure the various goals and make identifications, suggestions, and corrections

» Design and implement appropriate programs capable of treating and correcting fitness deficiencies

» Work with disabled individuals in developing fitness programs

Physical Fitness Trainer   City, State   2004–2006.

» Guided clients in various fitness programs, including stretching, bending, range of motion, and strengthening exercise

  » Assisted staff with fitness testing

  » Administered assessment testing

  » Maintained client files and facility upkeep

Volunteer Work

  » Hospital: physical fitness and recreational therapy

» University and Town Health Center: outpatient physical fitness

  » Boy's and Girl's Clubs of America: overview of programs

Memberships

  » American College of Sports Medicine (Fellow)

  » National Strength and Conditioning Association

» National Association for Health Fitness and Physical Training

  » American Association of Things Benefiting Society

References

Available Upon Request

Résumé Example 4. Mid-Level Employment, BA, Ten Years' Experience.

Carol C. Clark
246 Park Avenue
City, State 35790
333-456-7890
ccc@swick.com_Investment Advisor—Domestic and International_

Asset Management, Financial Assistance, Strategic Development,
Public Relations, World Banking, Foreign Exchanges, Short- and Long-Term Lending,
Investment Development, Portfolio Development, Portfolio Advisement

Highly motivated, independent-thinking, goal-oriented professional with a proven track record seeking a position as an investment manager, preferably in an international setting. My record of success involves investment planning, market analysis, and world banking exposure, in both the US and European markets. Superior recruitment and retention rates of clients in both the investment and banking industry, also excellent high production rates worldwide.

Completely bilingual in English, Spanish, and Italian. Will travel as necessary.

Experience

Investment Advisor, Executive Vice President

World Investment Group   City, State   2006–present

- » Develop and maintain investment relationships with clientele both domestic and international
- » Develop and maintain a total $10 billion portfolio for the international clientele
- » Analyze client portfolios to make suggestions for various options in a portfolio
- » Predict current financial strategies with a goal of improving financial gains

» Direct various development teams (both as a member and as a leader) for expansion of the World Investment Group

» Developing partnerships with numerous firms for increased revenue

Investment Sales Manager

Regional Bank, Investment Services   City, State   2004–2006

» Secured, assimilated, and established credible investment associations with historically successful firms on both a national and international level

» Strategically analyzed financial portfolios for team members to advise clients of their needs.

» Provided sound solutions to clients' personal investment portfolios

» Managed investment portfolios of over $100 million for 60 clients on a daily basis

» Consistently surpassed sales goals with clients through development of positive relationships and affective communications

» Developed strategic models to assist other branch teams reach goals and objectives

Investment Sales Advisor

Area Bank, City, State   2002-2004

» Consistently ranked in the top 10% of sales and commissions received for five consecutive years

» Directed investment portfolios totaling over $20 million consisting of stocks, bonds, currencies, and commodities. Increased these investment portfolios with an average gain of @ 16%.

» Involved in company research and design to advance and maintain numerous portfolios

» As a result of effective marketing skills, developed and maintained new relationships resulting in a successful increase of 21% in profits

Trust Associate

State Bank   City, State   2002-2004

» Scheduled training with bank personnel and trust officials for increased efficiency.

» Coordinated conferences with clients and advisors for investment.

Education

BA, Business Administration, Investment Major, Sociology Minor

City College of State, School of Business   City, State   1998-2002

Professional Licenses

Securities and Exchange Commission Certificate of Sales

State Insurance License

Annuities License

References will be furnished upon request.

Résumé Example 5—Mid-Level Employment, Little Education vs. More Experience

Arthur A. Ashburn
2345 Pennsylvania Avenue
City, State 57953
333-345-6543
aash@tjse.com

Strong Highly Accomplished Executive—Nautical Development and Design

Strengths Include

Human Resource Management and Direction • Tactical Planning and Execution • Teamwork Expansion • Educational Planning • Cross-Cultural Cohesion • GFD Auditing and Appraisal • Governmental Regulations and Relationships • Training and Advancement • Development of Client Satisfaction • Strategic Organization

Some of My Accomplishments Include

» A record of within-budget, on-time project execution leading to significant monetary gains in all areas of implementation has been my consistent MO.

» Solid experience in administration and management has, on one project alone, led to an increase of 23% in production and an increase of 46% in revenue.

» Design, implementation, and direction of one US Navy contract gained approval in five short months and also resulted in a 19% increased revenue not previously anticipated.

» Highly organized and able to produce within time restraints and budget requirements—in fact, our last three major contracts were completed under-budget and well within time requirements, resulting in 41% increased revenue.

> » Extremely conscious of overall customer satisfaction, quality, and efficiency to the extent of receiving "Outstanding Customer Approval" awards from the Nautical Business Bureau and Association for three years in a row.

Professional Experience

Director of Nautical Quality and Inspection
Nautical Developers, Inc.   City, State   2005 to Present

> » As a key director, assume major responsibilities and duties for complete operation of the company and expansion thereof

> » Manage all nautical inspection and repairs directly coming into company

> » Auditor of all inside and outside revenues

> » Responsible for safety programs, implementation, and development

> » Coordinator of customer satisfaction and inquiries

> » Expedite customer requests and selection of new and additional products

> » Supervise all regulations concerning company repair and operations

Head, Nautical Design and Implementation
Boat Builders, Inc.   City, State   2000 to 2005

> » Mechanical inspection and correction of nautical defaults

> » Training and development of employees

> » Coordinated various programs for installation and operation of facilities

> » Developed outreach programs for customer assistance

Boat Engine Mechanic
Boat Company   City State   1998 to 2005

> » Performed daily mechanical repairs and operations

> » Assembled nautical engines and boat configurations

> » Inventoried nautical accessories and components

Mechanic

Company

> » Performed simple boat engine repair

> » Assembled simple boat engines

Education

County Community College   City, State   1994-1998
Associates Degree (AS), Automotive Mechanics

Diploma   City, State   1990-1994
Garden Ceramic High School (Automotive Degree)

Licenses and Certifications
Certification of Completion at the Nautical Mechanic Association of America.
City, State 10/2001
Certification of Mechanical Training
City, State 6/2000

References Will Be Furnished Upon Request

Résumé Example 6—Mid-Level Employment, Different Experiences in One Industry

Rachael Reuben

5790 Park Avenue

Anytown, Anystate 33909

567-890-1234

rreu@tjse.com

Objective

Multiplicity and Corporate Growth Administrator

My Strengths Include:

Design of Business Environment and Image • Development of Training and Leadership • Recruitment and Retention of Personnel • Assembling of Efficient Work Groups with Diverse Representation • Delivering Guidance and Direction at All Operation Levels • Providing Recognition and Reward for Employee Achievement • Reorganization and Company Upgrading • Sensitivity Training and Cooperation • Development and Use of a Company Vision Statement • Involvement and Support in Community Affairs

My Accomplishments Include:

» A positive track record that in one instance alone advanced and maintained a diverse and innovative enterprise affecting more than 3,500 employees and resulting in a 49% increase in total production

» Most recent project for my company resulted in more than a $1,500,000 increase in gross sales and revenues within an 18-month period of time, highlighting my abilities as a problem-solver and decision-maker

» Strong communication skills and effective interpersonal relations allowing me to develop numerous programs resulting in increases in production and revenues in many instances, e.g. the Westing Homelight Project and the Omar Tent-Making Venture.

» Use of personal mentoring, mediation, and negotiation skills that have led to growth and development in all areas of company involvement, each resulting in increased efficiency, productivity, and profitability

Fluent in English, French, Russian, Swahili
Will travel as necessary

Professional Experience

Vice President, Regional Director of Development
Large Corporation   Large City, State   2002 to present
» Application and direction of various strategic actions within the corporate structure to improve efficiency by 22%

» Organization of a sensitivity group to include over 500 employees, 10 countries, and all entities to increase communication between employees in various countries with an increase beyond measurement

» Endorsed, cultivated, and assisted in the presentation of e-learning awareness and communication training and workshops, creating increased productivity of 18%

» Developed employee sensitivity and appreciation of cultural diversity within the group 10% yearly by use of a Cultural Temperament and Appreciation Survey

» Increased diversity cognizance between cultural groups by creating responsiveness via interaction and participation in activities between the cultural groups

» Promoted diversification interest and participation through involvement in various activities, such as Red Cross Volunteers, March of Dimes, Disaster Relief, and Race for the Cure by 26%

» Acted on behalf of country in various diversity settings to increase participation, contribution, and fulfillment in awareness programs and functions throughout the total community.

» Joined and contributed as an executive member in the development and advancement of country appreciation for continued growth and increased profits of approximately 47%.

Business Corporate Officer
Big Corporation—Sales and Manufacturing   1996–2002

» Achieved significant increase in client participation to include an increase in revenue of $50,000 and a decrease in attrition of 22%

» Increased relationships of client satisfaction and gross revenues by diverse marketing procedures resulting in 42% revenue increase

» Sustained and surpassed previous production and revenues by 28%

Relationship Manager
Corporation—Retail Sales   City, State   1990–1996

» Attained effective customer services for all areas of the company resulting in 50% increase in new products with increased sales never before realized

» Achieved and exceeded weekly, monthly, and annual production targets by over $500,000 in total revenue increases

Education

Big Time University   City, State   1984–1990
Master of Business Administration, 1990
Bachelor of Arts, 1988

Professional Associations

» Women's Association of Business and Profession Achievement

» Corporate and Industry Advancement (secretary/treasurer)

» Foundation of Corporate Advancement (vice president)

» Woman's Council (board member 2006 to present, member 2002)

References Available Upon Request

Résumé Example 7–Executive Level, Highest Level of Experience

Marcus Wellbeing

M.D., M.B.A.

2468 49th Street, NW

New City, New State 14702

202-220-2020

marcuswell@tjse.com

Hospital Director, Hospital Manager, Senior Director, Operations, and Management
My Strong Points Include:

Development, Direction, and Planning • Ongoing Education and Training for All Staff and Employees • Recruitment and Retention • Overseeing All Budgets and Controls • Direction of Project Management • Development, Administration, and Supervision of Warehousing Supply and Distribution • Development and Direction of Capital Improvements • Cost and Competitive Analysis Research and Increase of Grant Awards • Growth and Development of Patient Education • Advancement and Promotion of Outpatient Clinics.

My Accomplishments Embrace:

» Successful management of total hospital operations with the responsibility for over 700 employees, 3,500 patients, and a multi-million-dollar budget. In the first year alone, we realized a growth of 19% with an efficiency gain of 17% in operation.

» Outstanding motivational skills that have coordinated quality care systems for logistic improvements, process improvements and activities, cost reduction without care reduction, and improved employee relations, which in turn provided improved patient care. Total increase in participation of staff and employees exceeded 50%.

» Reorganizing and redistributing of budget to improve total health-care in all areas of the hospital. Additional programs increased from seven to seventeen in number.

» Developed a preventive health-care system to include fitness centers, assessment centers, and personal fitness centers. Initial enrollment started at 150 patients and has already grown to 410 and rising.

» Responsible for establishing patient education for personal health as well as the necessary requirements for preventative health. Tremendous results have been established thus far, with benefits reportedly received by everyone involved.

» Directly responsible for planning and expansion of over $59,000,000 in capital improvement. Phase 1 is now completed, with Phase 2 presently in progress.

Experience

Hospital Director, Operations Manager, Department Manager
New Hospital   New City, New State   2002-2011

» Managed total operation of New Hospital with responsibility for 700 employees, 3,500 patients, and a multi-million-dollar budget

» Responsible for new facility construction and equipment installation, along with approval of design and specifications

» Developed quality improvement systems, logistic facilitation for patient care, and cost reduction in treatment while at the same time maintaining quality and service

» Planned schedules for complete operations to include all aspects of hospital functions

Key Accomplishments:

» Strong management and interpersonal skills to the extent of establishing successful cooperative, productive, and professional teams for the total operations of the hospital

» Successfully launched seven new programs to improve hospital services, providing patient care in various areas of patient education

- » Developed and administered a total operating budget of more than $550,000,000

  - » Prepared and utilized plans that eliminated waste by 17%

  - » Stayed under operating budgets by approximately 11%

Medical Officer, Head of Emergency, Surgical Director

City Hospital   City, State   1996-2002

- » Managed effective emergency-room services to include service to patients, alacrity of care, and effectiveness of budget with operational constraints

- » Increased relationships between emergency-room services and total hospital functions for increased productivity and effectiveness of 19%

- » Improved and maintained total productivity and effectiveness by 11%

Emergency-Room Physician

City Hospital   City, State   1994-1996

- » Provided effective patient emergency-room services on an as-needed basis

- » Improved coordination of emergency-room facilities and services

- » Expanded emergency-room services to increase patient needs

Education

Ivy League School   City, State

Master of Business Administration, 2000 Doctor of Medicine, 1994, with Honors State University, City, State Bachelor of Science, 1990, Magna Cum Laude

Professional Affiliations

- » American Medical Association

- » American Emergency Room Physicians (fellow)

- » Society for Development of Patient Medical Education

- » State Society for Medical Affiliation (founder, 2001)

References Will Be Furnished Upon Request

Résumé Example 8—Executive Level, Broadcast Media

Walter C. Cronklet   **1357 Flatbrush Avenue**   **Anybrook, Anystate**
10506 212-323-4344   wallet@tjse.com

Objective

Administrative-Level Radio and Television Broadcast Media

EXECUTIVE PROFILE:

Media career with progressive experiences developing innovative marketing to present radio and television programs worldwide. Expertise combines creative design, strategies, and leadership coupled with strong management, expansion, and economic capabilities.

ACHIEVEMENTS INCORPORATE:

» Improved and advanced broadcast market media for present local television agency in three short years. Results accounted for 31% in revenue growth and 44% in marketing growth.

» Advanced contract marketing communications and market positioning awareness resulting in sales growth of over 66% in local sales and 29% in nationwide sales.

» Developed executive-level presentations for inclusion of industry leaders to become aware of market trends and increased market analysis. Results included significant improvement on both the local, national, and international level.

» Created a client marketing increase resulting in new business development to the extent of 43%, increasing total revenue realized by more than $575,000.

» Specialized in management by design to encourage developing, advancing, and maintaining programs that involve all participants engaged in the promotion of the industry. Results have thus far been received with great enthusiasm.

» Coordinated the management of these programs by design, allowing for an increase in listener audiences by 39%. Within one short year, the revenue increase exceeded $4,000,000.

STRONG POINTS INCLUDE:

Radio and Television Broadcast Media • Client Marketing Coordination • Media Positioning and Analysis • Sales Presentations and Promotions • Executive Media Presentations • Client Broadcast Marketing • New Broadcast Marketing • Retention of Broadcast Marketing • Management of Broadcast Relationships • Staff and Team Development and Leadership • Timely and Within-Budget Delivery • Corporate Vision and Strategy • Research and Future Design • Implementation of Cross-Cultural Sensitivity Training

Multilingual Fluency in English, Spanish, German, and Swahili

PROFESSIONAL EXPERIENCE

Executive Vice President

Anybrook Television Station, Anybrook, Anystate, 2000 to present

A full-service radio station offering advertising, public relations, marketing, communications, and informational services throughout the market. Recognized as one of the countries outstanding leaders.

Senior Vice President

Company Television Station, Anybrook, Anystate, 1996–2000

Began as account manager and account supervisor. Promoted to senior vice president, manager, and supervisor after one year, with responsibility for client satisfaction and representation.

Vice President

National Agency, Otherbrook, Otherstate, 1988–1996

Joined company as an account manager. Promoted to vice president in one year. Established a reputation as a corporate-identity specialist.

Project Manager

Station, City, State, 1984–1988

Represented station as service manager and then project manager.

Account Executive

Company, City, State, 1982–1984

Worked in advertising with a budget for recruitment of new business.

EDUCATION

University of Region   City, State   1980-1982

Masters in Media Management

Greater University   City, State   1976-1980

Bachelor of Science in Marketing

MEMBERSHIPS

National Association of Media Managers

American Association of Radio and Television Production

Kiwanis Club International (president)

References Will Be Furnished Upon Request

Résumé Example 9—Executive Level, Corporate President

Helen H. Helper, DBA
4578 South Street, SW
Southern city, Southern state 30123
675-765-5670

A dynamic, self-motivated senior administrator—with a commendable career in administration, supervision, management, development, organization, and direction—seeking a position in which my education, experience, and background can be utilized to the fullest.

Assets Include:

Strategic Planning and Development • Technical Planning and Development • Divisional Structuring and Reorganization • Program Cost Reduction • Labor Contract Negotiation • Diversity Sensitivity • Development of Benefit Packaging.

Experience

Vice President, Sales and Marketing

Special Products Services, Inc.   City, State   2002-2011

Special Products Services, Inc., is one of the largest companies manufacturing special products in the US and Canada. Their mission centers around providing special services to those with need in both countries without compromising quality, economy, or delivery.

Responsibilities include:

» Negotiate effective rates on all products and services

» Oversee quality production of all products and services

» Analyze ratio between production and negotiation

» Review cost effectiveness and delivery of products

» Coordinate activities between all producers and providers

Accomplishments include:

» Established and expanded department efficiency over 25% in first year alone

» Update delivery of services to provide results in three days or less

» Analyzed delivery processes resulting in $50,000 increased profit per week

» Developed and implemented methods of production resulting in 37% increased revenues

» Received highest recognition for professional presentation and direction from the American Association of Special Producers in the year 2010

Manager, Sales and Marketing

Somewhere Product Services   City, State   1996-2002
Accomplishments included:

» Implemented procedures to improve product services

» Initiated new projects increasing efficiency by 46%

» Maximized delivery input resulting in $25,000 average saving per month

» Designed procedures in delivery which resulted in 27% increase.

Education

University of New State   City, State
Doctor of Business Administration   2002
College of State   City, State
Bachelor of Business Administration   1990

Certification and Affiliations

» Certified Public Delivery of Products and Services

» North American Society of Planners and Developers

» Registered Producer of Products and Suppliers

References Will Be Furnished Upon Request

Profile Example 1–Recent College Graduate, Accounting Position with No Work Experience

John J. Jones 1234 Any Street Any Town, USA 421-445-4545 jones@gmail.com

Statistical Accounting/Programming

Very professional college graduate; quality-, efficiency-, diligence-minded in areas of statistical analysis and referencing; analytical accounting and programming; analytical reasoning and design; systems accounting.

Education

Bachelor of Science in Statistical Accounting and Programming, 2011

Computer Skills

Microsoft Word, Microsoft Office, Excel, Fortran, STS,
Windows, Word, Web Design, Microsoft Office.

Experience

Personal/Accounting Assistant. Assistant to Store Manager. City, State 2006–2011
Professional Student Advisor. Teaching of Computer Skills.
Development of Personal Accounting Skills Programs. 2004-2006
Assistant Manager for Office Designs. Responsible for Stock Inventory.
Worked in conjunction with school attendance. 2002-2004.

Call for references.

Profile Example 2–Recent PhD Graduate, Entry Level with Work Experience

John Clark
234 South Street
City, State 34567
JohnC@hotmail.com
456-367-6789

Developmental and/or Rehabilitative Exercise Physiologist
Highly motivated exercise physiology doctoral candidate with successful program development, rehabilitation coordination, and facilitation. Emphasis on overall fitness for prevention of future diseases.

Education
University of State, City, State. PhD in Exercise Physiology 2012
City College, City, State. MS Biology (emphasis on human anatomy and physical therapy)
Graduated Magna Cum Laude

Experience:
Internships in Physical Fitness

References will be furnished upon request.

APPENDIX B

Motivating Letters

Motivating Letter 1—Application for Entry-Level Job in Accounting

Mr. John C. Character
Superior Accounting Firm
2468 State Street
Any town, USA 01235
jjjones@switch.com

1234 Any street
Any town, NY 01234
Any date, Anytime
555-555-5555

Dear Mr. Character:

As a relatively new college graduate with a reputation for quality, efficiency, and diligence, I am seeking a position that will make good use of my skills and talents. My employers' and professors' praise of my work speaks to my potential for excellence.

Throughout my college career, I have demonstrated outstanding ability and aptitude in such areas as statistical referencing; analytical accounting and reasoning; system accounting and programming; project design; and leadership. At that time, while working a 20-hour week, I was also able to compile a 3.5 grade-point average.

My employer had this to say about me at my most recent part-time job:

> *During the time John worked with us, I could always count on him doing a quality job. He went well beyond what was asked of him and made a very positive, significant contribution to our company.—Susan, Store Manager, Department Store, Dallas*

The most recent opening with your company for an entry-level accountant looks very attractive. I would certainly appreciate the opportunity to interview with you and/or provide any additional information or clarification if so desired.

May I please hear from you? Until then I remain ....

Very truly yours,

John J. Jones

Motivating Letter 2—Recent College Graduate, Entry Level with Intern Work Experience

Mr. Carl Somebody, President
Quality Engineering Company
1357 State Street
City, State 09753
Cell: 555-555-5555

123 Main Street
Central University Dorm
Atlanta, GA 30353
sjohnson@hos.com

Dear Mr. Somebody:

As a soon-to-graduate engineering major (BS–MS Combination in June 2012 from Central University), I am seeking the position you have available with your company as an architectural engineer with environmental emphasis. My record of accomplishment includes a very successful completion of coursework and internships with a total grade-point average of 3.5.

In a very short period, during full-time summer internships, I have established a reputation for improving quality, efficiency, and client satisfaction. These personal skills and experiences would add a great deal to your successful company. Also during my college career, key achievements were completed in designing and implementing ADA regulations for new building construction.

As an environmental-engineering intern with the Engineering Associates of Some State from May through August 2005, I accomplished and completed projects to the company's satisfaction in areas including

- » wind and water erosion,
- » reinforced design for environmental protection, and
- » evaluation of various conditions for ADA compliance.

Additionally, I had the responsibility for coordination of a final printing on a special environmental project.

As a result of my experience, I have developed the following strengths: 1) manual and computer documentation; 2) environmental research and design; 3) ADA compliance; 4) environmental testing; 5) quality environmental assurance; and 6) governmental agency regulations.

If your company is seeking a self-motivated, enthusiastic, dedicated team player, I would be more than happy to meet with you and/or provide further information as desired.

May I please hear from you?

Sincerely yours,

Samuel Johnson

Motivating Letter 3—Recent PhD Graduate, Entry Level with Work Experience

Dr. Bern Filler, Director
University Hospital Health Center
5678 University Boulevard
City, State 35790

234 South Street
City, State 34567
johnc@hotmail.com
456-567-6789

Dear Dr. Filler:

Your recent advertised position of Director of Health and Fitness Coordination sounds very attractive indeed. With a PhD in Exercise Physiology (May 2012), I have very pertinent education, experience, and background to offer that will help in the development, progress, and maintenance of your total overall programs at the University Hospital Health Center.

My personal research presently includes "Rehabilitation of Knee Injuries" and "Improvement of Chronic Pulmonary Disease." These are two of what I consider to be important topics in individuals regain, maintain, and improve Health & Fitness. Through these programs, we provide the proper activities that will make available a Quality of Life that is complete, beneficial, and worthwhile.

As a student, I graduated with high honors in my Master's degree and have maintained a GPA of 3.6 in my Doctoral studies. My graduate courses and interests have included: Advanced Physiology of Exercise, Kinesiology, Biomechanics, Physiological Psychology, Psychometrics, Research and Design. More than anything, my wish is to work with people and help them improve their personal Quality of Life. *As a result of my experience, I have developed significant strengths in:*

1. *Programs for Chronic Pulmonary and Heart Disease Intervention*
2. *Coordination of Athletic Injury and Surgery Rehabilitation*
3. *Facilitation of Programs for Daily Functioning of Disabled Individuals*
4. *Assisting Members Achieve Personal Goals in the Health and Fitness Program*

If your program or plans call for an ambitious, friendly, hardworking individual such as my-self, I would be more than delighted to meet with you and/or provide further information or clarification as desired. May I please hear from you? Until then I remain …

Very truly yours,

John Clark, Doctoral Candidate

Motivating Letter 4—Mid-Level Employment, BA with Ten years' experience.

246 Park Avenue
City, State 35790
333-456-7890
ccc@swick.com

Mr. Alberto A. Aquilla, President
Costa Rican Aura Group
9988 San Joaquin Blvd.
San Jose, Costa Rica

Mr. Aquilla,

My successful record as a highly motivated, independent-thinking, goal-oriented professional with a superior record in investment management makes me a perfect fit for your recently announced position as an Executive Director of Investment Banking. Being completely bilingual in English, Spanish and Italian, along with ten years of excellent, successful experience, would allow me to make a very positive input and contribution to your company.

For example, as a result of my recent direction of and involvement with associates and staff, my present company realized a significant 22% increase in recruitment and retention rates in both the investment and banking areas.

In another instance, I have been instrumental in developing and maintaining investment relationships with clientele both domestic and international. As a direct result of my input, the company I was working with realized an appreciation of over $400,000 gain in profit per portfolio.

Utilization of my experience and background would be instrumental in advancing and maintaining the goals and objectives of the Costa Rican Aura Group. If your programs or plans call for a successful, eager, self-starting individual, I would be delighted to provide additional information or clarification as necessary.

May I please hear from you? Until then, I remain,

Very truly yours,

Carol C. Clark

Motivating Letter 5—Mid-Level Employment, Light Education and with More Experience

2345 Pennsylvania Avenue
City, State 57953
333-345-6543
aash@tjse.com

Mr. John Paul Jones, Director
Oceanic Nautical Associates
1357 Starboard Street
Lake Weterwater, State 22234

Dear Mr. Jones:

The purpose of this letter is to make application for your recently announced position as Manager of Nautical Resources with Oceanic Nautical Associates. As a strong executive in the nautical field, I have over thirteen years of pertinent experience and successful accomplishments.

My background includes a strong history in:

- » *Human Resource Management and Direction*
- » *Tactical Planning and Execution*
- » *Teamwork Expansion*
- » *Educational Planning*
- » *Cross-cultural Cohesion*
- » *GFD Auditing and Appraisal*
- » *Governmental Regulations and Relationships*
- » *Training and Advancement*
- » *Development of Client Satisfaction*
- » *Strategic Organization*

During my work history, I have established a significant record in the field of nautical operations. For example, with a strong amount of experience in Nautical Administration and Management, I completed one of many projects that led to an increase of 23% in production and an increase of 46% in revenue. In another instance, as a direct result of my design, implementation, and direction, my present company completed a U.S. Navy contract in five short months and returned a 19% increase in revenue not previously anticipated.

Your position as Manager of Nautical Programs along with the reputation of your company in total, most certainly looks attractive, challenging, and rewarding. I would be delighted to be considered for the position and/or to provide further information or clarification as desired. May I please hear from you?

Until then, I remain,

Very truly yours,

Arthur Ashburn

Motivating Letter #6–Mid-Level Employment, Different Experiences in One Industry

5790 Park Avenue
Bend, OR 97702
567-890-1234
rreu@tjse.com

Dr. James B. Pouton, Chairman
American-European Diversity Researchers
1429 Discovery Circle

Geneva, Switzerland M464GS

My Dear Dr. Pouton:

As a highly successful developer of diversity training, I am very much interested in your company's recent position as Executive Director of Diversity Development and Advancement. My education, experience, and background speak for themselves, with a proven record of design, coordination, training, and leadership.

In one instance alone, advancement was made by my direct efforts to develop and maintain a diverse and innovative enterprise that affected more than 3,500 employees in ten different countries, resulting in a more than 49% increase in total production. The enterprise is still in operation today, and with the additions and improvements on my part, production and revenue increases are greater than expected.

As a very effective problem-solver, resourceful motivator, and decision-maker, I directed another recent project that netted a $1,500,000 increase in gross sales and revenues within a brief eighteen-month period. This diversity program of educational training and cultural appreciation has produced rewards for my company never before thought possible.

My strong communication skills and effective interpersonal relationships have allowed me to develop numerous programs resulting in increases of production and revenues. If you are seeking a highly motivated, self-starting, energetic individual to advance and maintain your position, I would be delighted to meet with you and/or provide additional information or clarification as desired.

May I please hear from you? Until then, I remain,

Very truly yours,

Rachael Reuben

Motivating Letter #7—Executive Level,
Highest Level of Experience

2468 49th Street, NW
Washington, DC 200101
202-220-2020
marcuswell@tjse.com

Dr. J. Jacob Heimlich, Chairman
Director Selection Committee
Greater Hospital, Greater State 14777

Dear Dr. Heimlich:

As an executive with well over fifteen years' experience in hospital management and administration, I would appreciate your acceptance of this letter of application for your most recently announced position as director of Greater Hospital. My record of successful management and direction in hospital administration speaks for itself, and I am more than happy to provide these brief descriptions.

My most recent position involved successful management of the total hospital operation, with responsibility for over 700 employees, 3,500 patients, and a multi-million-dollar budget. In the first year alone, through my direction and leadership, we realized substantial growth and an efficiency gain in all operations. This has occurred successfully for every year of my tenure.

In another instance, again through my personal direction, input, and leadership, we developed a preventative health-care facility to include fitness centers, assessment centers, and personal fitness centers—each designed to diagnose and provide individual fitness levels for all individuals concerned with a quality of care second to none.

As you can see with these few examples, I have been involved in the development, direction, and successful completion of a number of quality programs. My education goes beyond the doctoral level (Doctor of Medicine) to an MBA, both from The Ivy League University. I would be happy to meet with you and or provide further information or clarification as needed.

May I please hear from you? Until then, I remain ....

Very truly yours,

Marcus Wellbeing, MD, MBA

Motivating Letter # 8–Executive Level, Broadcast Media

1357 Flatbush Avenue
Akron, OH 44306
234-323-4344
wallet@tjse.com

Mr. Johnny Carsonian, Director
The Radio & Television Network
1200 Avenue of the Americas
New City, NY 01967

Dear Mr. Carsonian:

As a seasoned executive in radio and television media, I am interested in your recently announced position for administrator of radio and television production. My vast media career encompasses extensive experience developing innovative marketing programs worldwide in both radio and television. More importantly, these experiences combine creative design strategies and leadership with strong management, expansion, and economic capabilities.

These capabilities have included the improvement and advancement of broadcast market media for present local agencies. Results accounted for 31% in revenue growth and 44% in market growth. All this took place in a period of three short years.

In another instance, I was responsible for the advancement of contract marketing communications and market positioning awareness. The result of my direct influence was a growth in sales of over 66% in local revenue and 29% in nationwide revenue.

Throughout my career, I have worked to develop a positive reputation embracing

» **client marketing enhancement and coordination,**

» **successful presentations in sales and promotions, and**

» **effective broadcast marketing.**

Additionally, I created staff and team-leadership development programs.

If your organizational plans call for an industrious, energetic, dedicated individual, please feel free to contact me for a meeting and/or to provide additional information or clarification as needed.

May I please hear from you? Until then I remain,

Very truly yours,

Walter C. Cronklet

Motivating Letter #9—Executive Level, Corporate President

4578 South Street, S.W.
Southern City, MS 39269
601-765-5670
help@tjse.com

Ms. Sally Savior, CEO
The Significant Company
1470 Madison Avenue, N.W.
Southern City, Southern State 30146

Dear Ms. Savior:

The purpose of this letter is to explore the possibility of joining your company in a position that would utilize my education, experience, and background to the fullest extent. Educated through the doctoral level (D.B.A. in Business Administration from The State University of New State), I also have some 20+ years of pertinent experience to offer.

Throughout my work history, I have demonstrated outstanding abilities as a dynamic, self-motivated, tireless executive. My successes have extended into the following fields:

»   strategic planning and development

»   technical planning and development

»   divisional structuring and reorganization

»   labor contract negotiation

»   diversified sensitivity training

»   development of benefits packaging

A few of my accomplishments have included the following:

- » **Established and expanded department efficiency over 25% per year**
- » **Updated delivery services providing results in three days or less**
- » **Modified delivery processes, increasing profits $50,000 per week**
- » **Developed and implemented methods of production resulting in 37% increased revenues yearly**

Although my present position is an agreeable one, I feel all of my talents and abilities are not being fully utilized. If your program or plans call for a highly motivated, tirelessly working, self-starting individual—if these are some of the things needed to advance and maintain a quality program—I would be happy to meet with you and/or provide further information or clarification as desired.

May I please hear from you? Until then I remain ………

Very truly yours,

Helen H. Helper, D.B.A.

APPENDIX C

Achievements and Accomplishments

This section provides you with an idea of what you can use to strengthen your application materials. Listing them in a positive way allows you to show in total all you have accomplished and achieved. Remember job descriptions do very little to present you in a favorable light as to what you have contributed to in any situations. You must show results ....*Accomplishments, Achievements, Contributions.*

Accomplishments: academics, scholarships, fellowships, honors, awards, distinctions, professional career achievements, professional recognitions

Affiliations: memberships, advisory boards, advisory committees, national boards, local boards, church committees, professional associations, professional organizations, professional societies, academic societies, honorary societies, committee membership, committee leadership

Education: overview, background, degrees, preparation, undergraduate degrees, master's degree (thesis title/topic), doctoral degree (dissertation title/topic), course focus and concentration, educational (knowledge, experience, expertise), interests and activities

Interdisciplinary: study abroad, interdisciplinary projects in marketing, research, and/ or design development, language proficiencies, career development and expansion. This is becoming more and more important in today's society.

Professional experience: professional growth and development, various appropriate experiences, areas of expertise, skills, proficiencies, various professional interests and participation, administrative experiences, grants and awards, contracts and patents

Professional training: fellowships, internships, fieldwork, specialized training, various certifications, licenses, professional certifications

Publications, seminars, workshops, presentations: attendance at conferences, presentations at conferences, leadership and organization, program organization, performances, recitals, editorial committees, reviews, articles, various professional, research, and technical papers

Teaching/research: assistantships, fellowships, appointments, teaching research, laboratory research, in-field research, awards, grants, projects, faculty leadership

APPENDIX D

Key Words

Keywords and how you use them can have a tremendous effect on your job search, the selection of your résumé in application for a job, and possibly the selection of you for the job. The keywords you use will make or break you in many situations. Keywords are easily found and can make you look like the person you want to be as far as the job is concerned. Choosing the correct keywords can surely put you in an excellent position. Remember the following:

>> Start with the job description and look for keywords that are used in the job description. For an accountant job, look for the keywords that describe that job—for example, "Perform a variety of general accounting support tasks in an accounting department."

>> Find out the tasks and keyword them. Look closely at the company. You can find information about the company throughout the Internet, even if it does not have a web page.

>> From the description of the company, locate keywords that are descriptive of the company and the job that interests you—for example, "Maintain accounting journals, prepare accounting reports, reconcile records."

>> Look up a job analysis in Google. Find out exactly what is the job description of an accountant. Use that description to identify keywords for the job analysis—for example, "Compile data and present reports."

>> In your own résumé that you developed, identify the keywords pertaining to the job description—for example, "Attention to detail and ability to multitask."

Specific Keywords

Accomplishment: achievement, deed, exploit, feat, success, triumph

Communication: announcement, consultation, contact, exchange, interaction, letter

Completion: achievement, attainment, carrying out, completion, execution, finishing, realization

Creative: artistic, exchange, imaginative, ingenious, innovative, inventive, original, productive, resourceful, statement, transmission

Detail: aspect, describes, element, facet, fact, factor, feature, itemize, list, point, specify

Financial: business, commercial, fiscal, monetary, pecuniary

Helping: abetting, aiding, alleviating, assisting, easing, facilitating, improving, relieving, serving

Management: administration, controlling, executive, organization, running, supervision

Research: examination, exploration, inquiry, investigation, seek, study

Skill: ability, capability, endowment, expertise, skill, talent

Technical: expert, mechanical, methodological, nominal, official, pedantic, practical, precise, practical, procedural, specialist, strict.

APPENDIX E

Questions to Prepare For

There are certain questions that tend to come up in a typical interview. Your interviewing technique would be enhanced by considering the nature of these questions.

Process-Related Questions

Most interviewees can say they did things like "developed and drove programs." It's difficult in this case to determine what the person's exact contribution was, especially when outside help was involved. You may be asked, "Tell me the process you used to develop the project" or "Describe the steps you took to complete the project." This is to your advantage if you use these questions to allow you to present the details of your role in a project.

You may also be asked this type of question to determine how you see yourself in the context of working with a team. Are you working with colleagues or simply assigning or completing various and numerous tasks? How are you interacting with your total management team? How are you making decisions and working to move projects forward?

Describe Your Best and Worst Jobs

This may be a very deceptive question if taken in the wrong context. Be absolutely certain in this case to pay close attention to how you talk about your interaction with other people. Did you clash with other people on your team? Sometimes you may be incompatible with someone on your team, but a repeating pattern of this type situation is suspicious. What were the aspects of the working relationships and culture at your jobs that you loved and hated?

Pay Attention to the Questions You Ask

When candidates ask a lot of questions about the work, they may think they appear more attractive. Actually, when they worry more about the organization, structure, and/or compensation in early interviews, they may appear less attractive. Generally speaking, good to excellent employees know that the job is the main thing. Compensation and titles are something to sort out after you know the job is a great fit for everyone concerned.

You may be asked to talk to lots of people in the company. Sometimes smaller companies are better at this than bigger companies. This is very much to your advantage, because you then realize if you indeed are interested in this particular company. The company's culture includes people with whom you will be working. If everyone can't get along with each other at the end of an interview, they sure won't be able to get along at the end of a workday or work week.

Often, a position will remain open for some time. Many candidates will have interviewed for the position and no candidate will be selected. It may mean the other people working in the situation are difficult themselves to get along with, so you must be diligent in your homework before accepting the job. If there's something irritating in the interview, it is almost guaranteed to make you uncomfortable later after acceptance of the job. Trust your instincts. If you feel something isn't quite acceptable and it can't be rectified, be warned.

Questions to Ask Yourself

These questions will help you get focused on the reasons you are seeking a new position. It is through this focus that you can best show yourself and the talents you have to your prospective employers. Remember, the better you can focus on the target or destination, the more attractive you will be to others. Unlike most job applicants, you will know where you want to go.

Be sure to invest enough time in answering the following questions so you get a crystal-clear vision of why you are seeking a new position:

» What specific objectives are you trying to achieve?

» Why are you writing this particular résumé? Are you looking for a new job, or a new position with the same employer?

» Are you trying to advance in your present job, move in another direction, or reenter the job market?

» What professional growth have you had along your career path?

» What is the highest level of education you have achieved? What is your degree, from what school, did you complete your studies, in what year, what was your major, and did you receive any honors?

» What was the title or topic of your master's thesis or doctoral dissertation, if any?

Some additional questions follow that could be important:

» What academic awards did you receive while in school?

» Do you hold any professional certifications or licenses?

» Do you have any special skills or qualities you could offer to a potential employer? How would these apply to the job you are seeking? Good examples would be foreign language, shorthand or note hand, and Internet skills.

» Do you belong to any professional associations? Have you held any offices or other positions in these associations? For recent college graduates, what organizations did you belong to, what teams were you active on, what volunteer work did you participate in?

» Have you ever published any work? List the titles, publication, or press.

» What prior jobs or positions have you held before this present one? Which did you get the most satisfaction and enjoyment from?

» Do you feel, up until this point, that your skills and accomplishments are stronger than your work experiences?

» How do you feel about relocating? Would you be willing to move yourself and/ or your family across country for a better opportunity?

» Are there any circumstances you would not like to include in your résumé? For example: being fired, gaps in your work history, major career changes, criminal record, eligibility, or availability for the job.

» List all of the jobs you have held in as much detail as possible, including the following information:

- the dates you worked in each position

- the specific responsibilities of the job and how these responsibilities carry over to the job you are seeking

- the successes you had, specifically—you managed, you developed, you motivated, you mediated, you wrote—and how each of these helped or benefitted your employer

- your contributions to advancing and maintaining the goals and success of the company or situation, using detailed examples and descriptions

- any advancements, awards, and promotions have you received along your career path to date, including any "Employee of the Quarter" type awards

» What would recommendations from past employers say about you? Are there any outstanding accomplishments you achieved or awards you received during your time on any particular job? What praiseworthy compliments did your get from your supervisors?

» In fifty words or less, why are you the best candidate for the job? What sets you apart from all of the other candidates? Be specific! Be concise! Be accurate! Be you!

» Are there any additional, particular, and specific skills you can bring to the job? Just what you are capable of doing?

Basic Skills

In today's complex, technology-driven society, everyone has some basic skills. These skills not only allow you to succeed in everyday living, they are the necessary skills you need for your profession. These skills include the following:

» *Technical skills*, very important in our life today, include those required for life in general as well as any specific technical skills required for your specific job.

Technical-skill development is an ongoing process, and successful people are consistently improving and upgrading their skills.

» *Interpersonal skills* are necessary to effectively deliver information, both verbally and nonverbally, to the people you communicate with both in and out of the job. To succeed at a high level of life and in your job, you need skills that include writing, speaking, presentation, communication, and management/leadership.

» *Psychological skills* help you demonstrate sincere concern, empathy, and interest in other people. Interaction with others is the key to psychological skill and includes the ability to help others develop and grow. This includes the ability to create harmony when working with others, the ability to know how to motivate others, and the ability to interact with others. If you possess psychological skills, you increase the motivation and energy around you, as well as your chances for success, happiness, and fulfillment in life.

ABOUT THE AUTHOR

Gerald N. Calandra, Ed.D, JD, has worked for over forty years in various areas of education. He started as a high-school biology teacher and swimming coach, and during his professional career has worked as a student advisor, high-school teacher, college professor, and in-house counsel. He taught in both high school and college while earning his Ed.D degree. After later receiving his JD degree, Dr. Calandra worked in various school districts as in-house legal counsel covering the countless areas of educational law.

Job-procurement methods have been a favorite and concentrated topic throughout Dr. Calandra's career. His written articles and numerous seminars on the subject of job-seeking have been well-received and praised by those at all levels of career placement and advancement. His personal education, experience, and background have contributed to a philosophy that brings a refreshingly *affective* and *effective* approach to the area of job searching. This has prepared his clients extremely well; by the completion of the program, they have acquired all the necessary skills to be job-seekers of the highest caliber.

N.B.: Additional information may be obtained by attending one of my Job Seeking Seminars. These seminars are held in various parts of the USA throughout the year. In session one, I spend approximately two to three hours lecturing completely on the materials covered in our manual. All aspects of the manual are covered with emphasis on individual attention to job seeking skills. In session two I spend two to three more hours working with you to aid in development of your own personal job seeking skills. None of our groups are more than 40 participants in size so that each individual gets the personal attention they need

My specially arranged consultations can also be scheduled and spent working individually with you on a one-to-one basis in development of skills for your total personal job seeking package.

Check with my website at www.jobseekingskills.com for further information and clarification.